The Open University

MT365 Graphs, networks and design

Networks 3

Assignment and transportation

Study guide

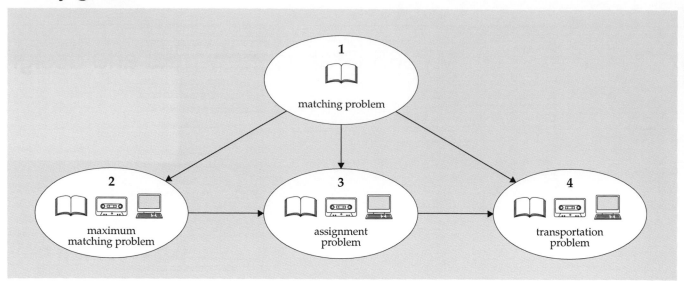

In Section 1 we set the scene by introducing matching problems. In each of Sections 2–4, we describe a standard optimization problem involving matchings and an algorithm which can be used to find a solution. Each of these three sections includes an audio-tape session and a computing activity.

The Open University, Walton Hall, Milton Keynes, MK7 6AA.

First published 1995. Second edition 2001. Reprinted 2002, 2003, 2005, 2006, 2009.

Printed and bound by Page Bros, Norwich.

ISBN 0 7492 3456 3

2.5

Contents

Introduction

The common feature of the network problems which we consider in this unit is that they can all be modelled by bipartite graphs. Some of these problems (such as the *marriage problem* introduced in Section 1) originated as problems in pure mathematics, whereas others (for example, the *transportation problem* discussed in Section 4) arose from practical problems in industry and commerce.

Most of the problems discussed in this unit are optimization problems for which we give methods of solution in the form of algorithms. The three basic optimization problems which we discuss — the *matching problem,* the *assignment problem* and the *transportation problem* — are closely related to the flow problems considered in *Networks 1* and can be solved by using the maximum flow algorithm. However, the algorithms given here are more efficient, since they make use of the fact that all the graphs involved are bipartite graphs.

In Section 1, *Matching problem,* we discuss the *marriage problem* and some related problems involving matchings in bipartite graphs.

In Section 2, *Maximum matching problem,* we consider problems in which we wish to find matchings in the corresponding bipartite graphs with as many edges as possible. We introduce the concept of an *alternating path,* and present an algorithm for finding a maximum matching based on this concept.

Section 3, *Assignment problem,* is concerned with assignment problems in which we have costs associated with the possible assignments and we wish to find matchings with least overall cost. The Hungarian algorithm which we give for solving this problem is based on the procedure used in the algorithm for finding a maximum matching. We also discuss a variation on the basic assignment problem, known as the *bottleneck assignment problem.*

In Section 4, *Transportation problem,* we discuss transportation and transhipment problems. The Hungarian algorithm for the transportation problem uses a similar procedure to the algorithm for the assignment problem.

1 Matching problem

1.1 Marriage problem

In this section we discuss some problems involving matchings in bipartite graphs. We begin by presenting three examples of the type of problem which we consider.

Example 1.1

Four jobs are to be assigned to four applicants. Applicant 1 is qualified to do only jobs A and B; applicant 2 is qualified to do jobs A, B, C and D; applicant 3 is qualified to do only jobs A and B; and applicant 4 is qualified to do only job B. Can all four applicants be assigned to different jobs for which they are qualified? ■

Example 1.2

Four men A_1, A_2, A_3 and A_4 each know some of four women B_1, B_2, B_3 and B_4. Man A_1 knows women B_1 and B_2; man A_2 knows all four women; man A_3 knows women B_1 and B_2; and man A_4 knows woman B_2. Is it possible for all the men to marry women they know? ■

Example 1.3

A company has four lorries and four depots. Lorry 1 can carry loads up to $1\frac{1}{2}$ tonnes; lorry 2 can carry loads up to 2 tonnes; and lorries 3 and 4 can each carry loads up to 1 tonne. Depot 1 needs a lorry to carry loads up to $1\frac{1}{2}$ tonnes; depot 2 needs a lorry to carry loads up to 1 tonne; depot 3 needs a lorry to carry loads up to $1\frac{1}{2}$ tonnes; and depot 4 needs a lorry to carry up to 2 tonnes. Can each depot be allocated a suitable lorry? ∎

In fact, all three examples can be expressed as exactly the same mathematical problem. This becomes obvious if we represent each situation by a graph. For Example 1.1, the following table shows the jobs for which each applicant is qualified. A graphical representation of this information is given on the right.

applicants	jobs
1	A, B
2	A, B, C, D
3	A, B
4	B

In the above graph, the black vertices represent applicants and the white vertices represent jobs. A black vertex is joined by an edge to a white vertex if the corresponding applicant is qualified to do the corresponding job. Since only vertices of different colours are joined, the graph is a bipartite graph.

If we represent Examples 1.2 and 1.3 by graphs in a similar way, we find that the graphs are identical to the one obtained above. For Example 1.2, we simply substitute 'men' for 'applicants', and 'women' for 'jobs'. For Example 1.3, we substitute 'depots' for 'applicants', and 'lorries' for 'jobs'.

Since the three problems are essentially the same, we restrict our discussion to the solution of Example 1.1.

As stated, each problem is an *existence* problem; the actual assignment is a *construction* problem.

Assigning an applicant to a job corresponds to choosing an edge of the bipartite graph. We can easily assign three of the applicants to different jobs; for example, we can assign applicant 1 to job A, applicant 2 to job D, and applicant 3 to job B.

This arrangement is shown in the following graph, where thick edges represent assignments of applicants to jobs.

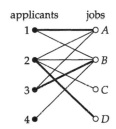

The pairing of some or all of the elements of one set with elements of a second set is called a **matching**. The matching represented by the thick lines of the above graph comprises the following pairings:

> applicant 1 with job A
> applicant 2 with job D
> applicant 3 with job B

A matching in a bipartite graph corresponds to a set of edges no two of which meet at the same vertex. The matching represented by the above graph contains three such edges, as shown by the thick lines.

A formal definition of a *matching* in a graph is given in *Graphs 3*. In this unit we are interested in matchings in *bipartite* graphs in which each edge of the matching joins a vertex in one set to a vertex in the other.

5

We now see that our original question:

> can all four applicants be assigned to different jobs for which they are qualified?

is equivalent to the question:

> can we find a matching containing four edges in the bipartite graph?

In fact, it is not possible to find such a matching in this graph. We say that the matching with three edges is a **maximum matching** — that is, it is a matching with the largest possible number of edges.

Problem 1.1

Suppose that four applicants apply for four jobs and that each applicant is qualified for some of these jobs, as shown in the following table.

applicants	jobs
1	A, D
2	A, B
3	A, B, C
4	B

(a)   Draw the bipartite graph which represents this situation.

(b)   By finding a maximum matching in the bipartite graph, find the maximum number of applicants that can be assigned to different jobs for which they are qualified.

In the above problem, it is possible for all four applicants to be assigned to jobs for which they are qualified. This is in contrast to our previous example, where at most three of the four workers can be assigned to different tasks for which they are qualified. For the general problem in which we are trying to allocate a set of applicants to various jobs, we should like to know under what conditions it is possible for all the applicants to be assigned to jobs for which they are qualified.

This problem was formulated in 1935 as a problem in group theory. It was later restated in terms of marriages, as in Example 1.2. For this reason, it is often called the *marriage problem*. We shall follow this tradition of discussing matching problems in bipartite graphs in terms of marriages, rather than in terms of more practical problems such as the assignment of workers to tasks or applicants to jobs. This has the advantage that it helps us to keep clear the distinction between matching problems and the related, but more general, assignment problems which we discuss in Section 3.

We state the marriage problem formally as follows.

Marriage problem

Given a set of men, each of whom knows some women from a given set of women, under what conditions is it possible for all the men to marry women they know?

It is assumed that each man can marry only one woman, and each woman can marry only one man.

One condition which must obviously be satisfied is that the total number of women must be equal to or greater than the total number of men. We can go further than this, and state that any two men must collectively know at least two women. More generally, for each subset of m men, the m men must collectively know at least m women, for all possible values of m.

This is a necessary condition for it to be possible for all the men to marry women they know. What is not so obvious is that it is also a sufficient condition. This result is known as the *marriage theorem*.

Theorem 1.1: marriage theorem

A necessary and sufficient condition for there to be a solution to the marriage problem (that is, for every man to be able to marry a woman he knows) is:

> for every subset of m men, the m men collectively know at least m women, for all values of m in the range $1 \le m \le n$, where n is the total number of men.

This theorem was proved (in a different formulation) by Philip Hall in 1935.

We prove this theorem at the end of this section. First, we examine how it applies to some specific cases.

We begin by applying the marriage theorem to Example 1.2. The following table shows which women are known to each of the four men.

men	women known
A_1	B_1, B_2
A_2	B_1, B_2, B_3, B_4
A_3	B_1, B_2
A_4	B_2

The marriage theorem states that for all the men to be able to marry women they know, the men in every subset of $\{A_1, A_2, A_3, A_4\}$ of size m must collectively know at least m women, for each possible value of m. This condition is known as the **marriage condition**.

So, to apply the condition systematically, we first list all possible subsets of men.

There are four men, so the total number of subsets is 2^4. However, we need look at only $2^4 - 1 = 15$ subsets, since we obviously do not need to consider the empty set.

The number of subsets of a set of n elements is 2^n.

The four men collectively know four women, so the marriage condition is satisfied for the subset $\{A_1, A_2, A_3, A_4\}$. The following table shows whether the marriage condition is satisfied for each subset of three men.

subset of men	women known	number of men m	number of women known	Is marriage condition satisfied?
$\{A_1, A_2, A_3\}$	B_1, B_2, B_3, B_4	3	4	yes
$\{A_1, A_2, A_4\}$	B_1, B_2, B_3, B_4	3	4	yes
$\{A_1, A_3, A_4\}$	B_1, B_2	3	2	no
$\{A_2, A_3, A_4\}$	B_1, B_2, B_3, B_4	3	4	yes

For the third of these subsets, the three men concerned collectively know only two women, so the marriage condition is not satisfied, and therefore all four men cannot marry women they know. For this example, we do not need to examine any more subsets, but if the marriage condition had been satisfied for all four subsets of three men, then we should have had to continue with the subsets containing two men, and if necessary, the subsets containing only one man.

Problem 1.2

Suppose that each of the three men A_1, A_2 and A_3 know some of the four women B_1, B_2, B_3 and B_4, as shown in the following table.

men	women known
A_1	B_1, B_3, B_4
A_2	B_4
A_3	B_2, B_3

(a)   Construct a table (similar to the one for the example in the text) showing for each possible subset of men, the number of men in that subset and the number of women the men collectively know. For each subset, indicate whether the marriage condition is satisfied. Use the table to decide whether it is possible for all three men to marry women they know.

(b)   If (in the general case) there are n men, how many subsets of men do you need to consider when applying the marriage theorem? Check that your answer for the case $n = 3$ agrees with the number of entries in your table.

(c)   Draw the bipartite graph representing this problem. Find a maximum matching in this graph corresponding to the maximum number of men who can marry women they know.

Problem 1.3

Consider four men A_1, A_2, A_3 and A_4 and four women B_1, B_2, B_3 and B_4. The following table shows which women are known to each of the four men.

men	women known
A_1	B_2
A_2	B_2, B_3
A_3	B_1, B_2, B_4
A_4	B_3

(a)   Draw the bipartite graph representing this situation.

(b)   Write down the subsets of men (if any) for which the marriage condition is not satisfied.

(c)   By inspection, find a maximum matching in the bipartite graph, and hence find the maximum number of men who can marry women they know.

So far we have been mainly concerned with the question posed by the marriage problem:

under what condition is it possible for all the men to marry women they know?

We have seen that this question is answered by the marriage theorem. When it is not possible for all the men to marry, it is natural to ask a second question, called the **modified marriage problem**:

what is the maximum number of men who can marry women they know?

In a practical version of this type of problem (such as assigning workers to tasks), we should probably be most interested in actually constructing a maximum matching. We express this problem as a third question:

how can we determine which man should marry which woman so that the maximum possible number of marriages can take place?

In the next subsection we shall be mainly concerned with the second question.

Our answer to the third question takes the form of an algorithm. We describe such an algorithm in Section 2.

1.2 Modified marriage problem

In the solution to Problem 1.3, we found by trial and error that of the four men A_1, A_2, A_3 and A_4, only three can marry women they know. We now show how to prove that the maximum number of men who can marry is three, without having to construct a possible scheme of marriages.

For convenience, we set out below a table and a bipartite graph showing which men know which women.

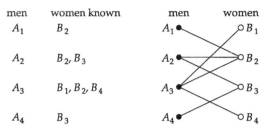

men	women known
A_1	B_2
A_2	B_2, B_3
A_3	B_1, B_2, B_4
A_4	B_3

We found in Problem 1.3 that the marriage condition is satisfied for all subsets of men except for the subset containing the three men A_1, A_2 and A_4, who collectively know only two women, B_2 and B_3. By the marriage theorem, it is not possible for all four of the men to marry.

Since the marriage condition breaks down because the three men A_1, A_2 and A_4 know only two women, it seems likely that if we remove one of these men, then the marriage condition will be satisfied for all possible subsets of the remaining three men. This is indeed the case. For example, if we remove A_1, then the subset $\{A_1, A_2, A_4\}$ becomes the subset $\{A_2, A_4\}$ and A_2 and A_4 collectively know two women.

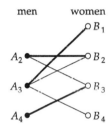

All the other subsets which contained A_1 and which previously satisfied the marriage condition still satisfy the marriage condition, so all three men can marry women they know. Although this is fairly obvious if we remove A_1, it is certainly not obvious that we can apply similar reasoning to a more complicated example.

Let us try another approach. Faced with a situation where the marriage condition was not satisfied, we converted the situation to one where the marriage condition was satisfied, by removing one of the men. However, we can also satisfy the marriage condition for all subsets of men by adding an extra women B_5, who is known by all the men. The men in the subset $\{A_1, A_2, A_4\}$ now know three women B_2, B_3 and B_5, and all the other subsets of men now know one more woman than before. Therefore, by the marriage theorem, all four men can marry women they know. If we now remove the extra woman B_5, we are left with three men who are married and one (the one who was married to B_5) unmarried. We have thus shown that it is possible for three of the men to marry women they know.

We now turn our attention to the general problem of finding the maximum number of men who can marry when the marriage condition is not satisfied.

If there are n men, then the marriage condition states that they can all marry women they know if

> (number of women known by each subset of m men) $\geq m$,
> for all values of m in the range $1 \leq m \leq n$.

If the marriage condition is not satisfied, we can write instead that $n - d$ men can marry women they know if

> (number of women known by each subset of m men) $\geq m - d$,
> for all values of m in the range $1 \leq m \leq n$, and for some positive integer d.

This is called the **modified marriage condition**. We prove this result by an argument similar to the one we used above for the example of Problem 1.3. All we have to do to prove the result is to add a group of d women who are known by all the men. With the enlarged group of women, the marriage condition is satisfied, so all the men can marry. Removal of the extra d women leaves $n - d$ men who are married, and d men who are not married. In other words, in the original problem, $n - d$ men can marry.

If we put $r = n - d$, we can write the modified marriage condition as:

> (number of women known by each subset of m men) $\geq m - (n - r)$,
> for all values of m in the range $1 \leq m \leq n$.

Note that if we put $d = 0$, then r is equal to n, and this condition reduces to the original marriage condition.

The maximum value of r for which this modified marriage condition is satisfied is the largest number of men who can marry women they know. We can rearrange the inequality in this marriage condition so that only r appears on the right-hand side:

> (the number of women known by each subset of m men) $+ (n - m) \geq r$,
> for all values of m in the range $1 \leq m \leq n$.

It is clear that the maximum value of r for which this condition is satisfied is equal to the minimum value of the expression on the left-hand side over all subsets of m men, over all values of m. We summarize this result in the following theorem.

Theorem 1.2: modified marriage theorem

If a group of n men each know some of a group of women, the maximum number of men who can marry women they know is equal to the minimum value of the expression:

> (number of women p known by a subset of m men) $+ (n - m)$,
> for any subset of m men, and for all values of m in the range $1 \leq m \leq n$.

This theorem is a minimax theorem, like the max-flow min-cut theorem and Menger's theorems in *Networks 1*.

In stating this theorem, we assume that the original marriage condition is not satisfied. Otherwise the minimum value of the expression may be greater than n.

Worked problem

Suppose that five men A_1, A_2, A_3, A_4 and A_5 know four women B_1, B_2, B_3 and B_4, as shown in the following table and bipartite graph. What is the maximum number of men who can marry women they know?

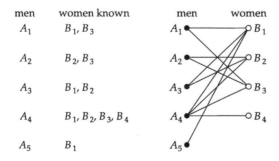

men	women known
A_1	B_1, B_3
A_2	B_2, B_3
A_3	B_1, B_2
A_4	B_1, B_2, B_3, B_4
A_5	B_1

Solution

To answer this question, we need to find the minimum value of the expression in the modified marriage theorem. To do this, we need consider only those subsets of men for which the original marriage condition is not satisfied. By inspection of the table or the graph, we see that there are only two such subsets: $\{A_1, A_2, A_3, A_5\}$ and $\{A_1, A_2 \ A_3, A_4, A_5\}$. We draw up the following table.

subset of men	women known	number of men m	number of women known p	$p + (n - m)$
$\{A_1, A_2, A_3, A_5\}$	B_1, B_2, B_3	4	3	4
$\{A_1, A_2, A_3, A_4, A_5\}$	B_1, B_2, B_3, B_4	5	4	4

For both subsets, the value of the expression $p + (n - m)$ is 4. Hence exactly four men can marry women they know. ∎

In the above worked problem, we found that at most four men can marry. The next question which arises is: which four of the five men can marry women they know? Or, to put it another way, which one man should we remove so that the remaining four can marry? To answer this question, we look at the two subsets for which the marriage condition is not satisfied. We must remove a man who is in both of these subsets. Clearly, there are four possibilities: A_1, A_2, A_3 or A_5. We remove each of A_1, A_2, A_3 and A_5 in turn, and find a marriage scheme for the remaining four men in each case. All such marriage schemes involving the maximum number of men (four) are shown below.

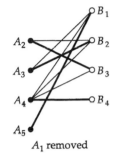

A_1 removed

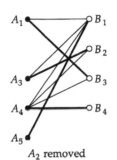

A_2 removed

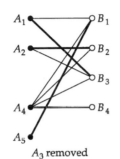

A_3 removed

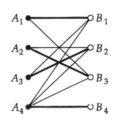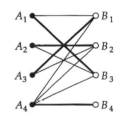

A_5 removed (two possibilities)

If A_4 is removed, then it is obvious that the remaining four men cannot all marry women they know, since none of them knows B_4.

Problem 1.4

Suppose that five men A_1, A_2, A_3, A_4 and A_5 know four women B_1, B_2, B_3 and B_4 as follows.

men	women known
A_1	B_1, B_3
A_2	B_2, B_3
A_3	B_2
A_4	B_3
A_5	B_1, B_2, B_4

(a) Show that the marriage condition is not satisfied.

(b) Draw a bipartite graph to represent this problem.

(c) List all the subsets of men for which the marriage condition is not satisfied.
For each of these subsets, find the value of the expression $p + (n - m)$ in the modified marriage theorem.

One way of doing this is to construct a table as in the solution to Problem 1.2. Alternatively, you may find the required subsets by inspection, using the graph representation.

(d) What is the largest number of men who can marry women they know? List all the subsets of men containing this number of men who can all marry women they know.

We have now answered the first and second of the three questions we listed earlier. The remaining question is:

how can we determine which man should marry which woman so that the maximum possible number of marriages can take place?

To answer this question, we might try to adapt the procedure based on the modified marriage theorem which we used in the solution to the previous problem. This procedure can be converted into an algorithm fairly easily, but such an algorithm is not very suitable for solving a practical form of the marriage problem in which, for example, we wish to assign a number of workers to tasks for which they are qualified. The method is unsuitable for the following reasons.

- Although the procedure tells us which subsets of men can all marry (or which workers can be assigned to tasks), it does not tell us which man should marry which woman. For small groups of men it is a fairly simple matter to construct a suitable marriage scheme, but for larger numbers we need a systematic method.

- The procedure is an exhaustion method which involves looking at all possible non-empty subsets of the set of n men. The number of such subsets is $2^n - 1$, which increases very rapidly as n increases. The time taken to perform an algorithm based on this procedure is therefore roughly proportional to 2^n, that is, to an exponential function of n. Since the time taken increases so rapidly with n, it would not be practicable to use the procedure for problems involving large values of n, even when using a computer.

- The procedure is wasteful, since it effectively carries out a search of all possibilities and finds all the subsets of men which contain the largest number who can marry (or the largest number of workers who can all be assigned to different tasks). In a practical situation, we normally require only one solution.

What we need is an efficient algorithm which constructs just one maximum matching. We describe such an algorithm in Section 2. Before doing this, we give two different proofs of the marriage theorem.

1.3   Two proofs of the marriage theorem

For convenience, we repeat the statement of the marriage theorem.

Theorem 1.1: marriage theorem

A necessary and sufficient condition for there to be a solution to the marriage problem (that is, for every man to be able to marry a woman he knows) is:

for every subset of m men, the m men collectively know at least m women, for all values of m in the range $1 \leq m \leq n$, where n is the total number of men.

Since it is obvious that the condition given in the statement of the marriage problem is necessary, we need prove only that it is sufficient. We prove this first by mathematical induction on n and then by a constructive proof.

Proof by mathematical induction

We carry out two steps.

STEP 1   *Verify that the theorem is true when $n = 1$.*

In this case, there is one man who knows at least one woman, so obviously the marriage problem has a solution.

By a constructive proof we mean a proof which actually shows how to construct a solution to a problem, as contrasted with a proof (such as a proof by induction) which establishes that a solution exists, but does not provide a procedure for finding one.

STEP 2   *Show that, if the theorem is true for every number of men less than n, then it must also be true for n men.*

We assume that the theorem is true for every number of men less than n. We consider n men. There are two cases which together cover all possibilities.

Case (a) Suppose that for all $m < n$ every set of m men collectively know at least $m + 1$ women.

In this case, the marriage condition is satisfied with 'at least one woman to spare' for every set of m men. We can therefore take any man and marry him to any woman he knows, and the marriage condition will still be satisfied for the remaining $n - 1$ men. By our assumption, the theorem is true for every number of men less than n, so it must be true for these $n - 1$ men. We can therefore marry off the $n - 1$ men appropriately. We have now married off all n men, so this completes Step 2 in this case.

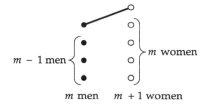

Case (b) Suppose that $m < n$ and that there is at least one set of m men who collectively know exactly m women.

From our assumption that the theorem is true for every number of men less than n, it follows immediately that we can marry these m men to the m women, leaving $n - m$ men and (since we are also assuming that the marriage condition is satisfied) at least $n - m$ women.

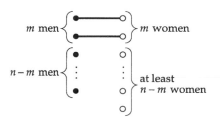

Now any collection of r men from these $n - m$ men must collectively know at least r women; otherwise these r men, together with the set of m men, would collectively know less than $r + m$ women, which is contrary to the marriage condition. It follows that, since we are assuming that the marriage theorem is true for fewer than n men, we can marry the remaining $n - m$ men to women they know. Thus, if the statement is true for all numbers of men less than n, then it is true for n men. This completes Step 2 in this case.

Therefore, by the principle of mathematical induction, the theorem is true for all positive integers n. ∎

Constructive proof

To prove that the marriage condition is a sufficient condition for there to be a solution to the marriage problem, we show that, starting with m men paired with m women (where $m < n$), it is possible to increase this to a pairing of $m + 1$ men. There is no difficulty in finding an initial pairing, since we can if necessary start with $m = 1$; that is, by pairing any man with a woman he knows. We can then successively increase the number of men paired until all n men are paired with women they know.

We begin with m men paired with m women whom they know.

If there is a man left who knows a woman not already paired, then an $(m + 1)$th pairing is immediately possible.

Otherwise, we proceed as follows.

We choose any unpaired man A_0. Since the marriage condition is satisfied, there must be at least one woman whom he knows — we choose one of these women B_1. Suppose that B_1 is paired with a man A_1. This pairing is indicated on the diagram by a thick line, and the fact that A_0 knows B_1 is indicated by the thin line joining the corresponding vertices.

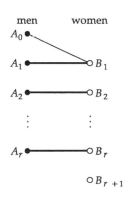

By the marriage condition, A_0 and A_1 must collectively know at least two women, namely, B_1 and at least one other woman B_2. If B_2 is not already paired, then A_1 must know B_2, so we pair A_0 with B_1 and A_1 with B_2 (removing the original pairing of A_1 with B_1); we thus obtain one more pairing, as required.

If B_2 is paired with A_2, then the men A_0, A_1 and A_2 must collectively know a third woman B_3. If B_3 is paired with A_3, we continue until an unpaired woman B_{r+1} is reached. A possible result of this procedure is illustrated on the left below.

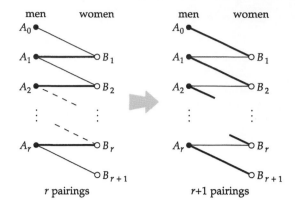

Note that each woman B_i involved in this process must be known by at least one man A_j, where $j < i$. This fact enables us to rearrange the pairings as follows. First we pair woman B_{r+1} with a man A_i who knows her (where $i < r + 1$). This frees woman B_i, who can be paired with some man A_j (where $j < i$). We continue in this way until a woman is free who can be paired with A_0. This process corresponds to tracing back a path which starts from B_{r+1} and proceeds by alternate thin and thick lines back to A_0.

We have now replaced the r original pairings in the above graph with $r + 1$ pairings. Together with the pairings not involved in this process, we now have a total of $m + 1$ pairings.

If there are still any men who are not paired (that is, if $m + 1 < n$), we continue with this process until all m men are paired with women they can marry. ■

The constructive process of the second proof provides a method for finding a matching of the n men to n of the women. The algorithm which we present for finding a maximum matching is based on the procedure of this proof.

After studying this section, you should be able to:

- explain the terms *matching, maximum matching* and the *marriage problem*;

- draw the bipartite graph representation of a marriage problem;

- state and use the marriage theorem and the modified marriage theorem.

2   Maximum matching problem

We now tackle the problem:

how can we find a maximum matching in a bipartite graph?

In this section we give an algorithm for finding such a matching. This algorithm is based on the concept of an *alternating path*.

2.1 Alternating paths

In the following bipartite graph, a matching M consists of the two edges $x_1 y_2$ and $x_3 y_3$ (indicated by thick lines). The diagram on the right illustrates an example of an *alternating path* with respect to M — only *alternate* edges of this path $x_4 y_3 x_3 y_2 x_1 y_1$ are edges of the matching M.

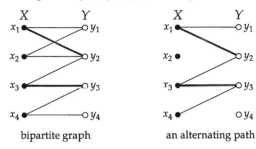

bipartite graph   an alternating path

There are three other alternating paths — the paths $x_2 y_2 x_1 y_1, x_2 y_1$ and $x_4 y_4$.

Definition

Let G be a bipartite graph in which the set of vertices is divided into two disjoint subsets X and Y. An **alternating path** with respect to a matching M in G is a path which satisfies the conditions:

(a)   the path joins a vertex x in X to a vertex y in Y;

(b)   the initial and final vertices x and y are not incident with an edge in M;

(c)   alternate edges of the path are in M, and the other edges are not in M.

It follows that the 1st, 3rd, 5th, ... edges are not in M, and the 2nd, 4th, 6th, ... edges are in M. Note that *an alternating path has odd length*.

Problem 2.1

Consider the following bipartite graph and matching M.

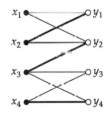

Which of the following paths are alternating paths with respect to M?

(a) $x_3 y_2 x_2 y_1$ (b) $y_3 x_3 y_2 x_2 y_1 x_1$ (c) $x_3 y_4 x_4 y_3$

Problem 2.2

Find all the alternating paths with respect to the matching shown in the following bipartite graph.

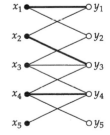

To see why the concept of an alternating path is useful for finding a maximum matching, consider the following diagrams.

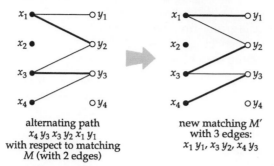

alternating path
$x_4 \, y_3 \, x_3 \, y_2 \, x_1 \, y_1$
with respect to matching
M (with 2 edges)

new matching M'
with 3 edges:
$x_1 \, y_1, \, x_3 \, y_2, \, x_4 \, y_3$

The diagram on the left shows our earlier example of an alternating path with respect to a matching M. In the diagram on the right, we have replaced the thick edges of the path by thin edges, and vice versa. In this way we have constructed a new matching M' consisting of three edges — one more edge than in the original matching M. It follows from the definition of an alternating path that if we can find an alternating path with respect to a matching M, then we can always construct a matching M' which has one more edge than M. The properties of an alternating path which ensure that this is the case are:

- for an alternating path with respect to a matching M, the number of edges of the path not in M is always one more than the number of edges of the path in M;

- the initial and final vertices of an alternating path are not incident with an edge in M.

In our example, the alternating path P includes all the edges of M. If the alternating path P does not include all the edges of M, the new matching M' consists of the edges of the alternating path P not in the matching M and the edges of the matching M not in the alternating path P.

For example, if we consider the alternating path $x_2 \, y_2 \, x_1 \, y_1$ with respect to the matching M in our bipartite graph, we obtain an improved matching as follows.

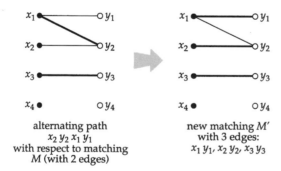

alternating path
$x_2 \, y_2 \, x_1 \, y_1$
with respect to matching
M (with 2 edges)

new matching M'
with 3 edges:
$x_1 \, y_1, \, x_2 \, y_2, \, x_3 \, y_3$

A formal statement of this procedure is given below.

To find a new matching with one more edge

Find an alternating path P with respect to an existing matching M.

Form a new matching M' with the following edges:

- the edges of the alternating path P not in the matching M

and

- the edges of the matching M not in the alternating path P.

2.2 Maximum matching algorithm

This method of using an alternating path to form a new matching is the basis of the following algorithm for finding a maximum matching.

To find a maximum matching, we start with a matching M, look for an alternating path P, and, if one is found, use it to construct a new matching with one more edge than before. We repeat the procedure until no more alternating paths can be found; the current matching is then a maximum matching.

We give a formal statement of the maximum matching algorithm and then work through an example in the first audio-tape session.

The algorithm is in two parts.

Part A is the labelling procedure for finding an alternating path.

Part B is the matching improvement procedure for finding a new matching with one more edge.

In the following audio-tape session, we illustrate the use of this formal algorithm by working through an example. Before listening to the tape, read through the statement of the algorithm given here. Have this statement and the *Audio-tape Notes* to hand when you listen to the tape.

This algorithm, in common with others presented in this unit, is written in a form suitable for implementing as a computer program. Its advantages may not be apparent from the small examples given in the tape, where the solutions can be quickly found by trial and error, but its usefulness is that it is a precise and systematic method which can be used to solve large examples with the aid of a computer.

Algorithm for finding a maximum matching

START   with any matching M in a bipartite graph whose sets of vertices are $X = \{x_1, x_2, ..., x_n\}$ and $Y = \{y_1, y_2, ..., y_m\}$.

> There is no difficulty in finding an initial matching M. If necessary, it can consist of just one edge.

Part A: labelling procedure

STEP 1   Label with (∗) each vertex in X which is not incident with any edge in the current matching M.

If no vertex in X can be labelled, STOP: the current matching is a maximum matching.

Otherwise, go to Step 2.

STEP 2   Choose a newly labelled vertex in X, say x_i, and label with (x_i) all the unlabelled vertices in Y joined to x_i by an edge NOT IN M.

Repeat this for all newly labelled vertices in X, and then go to Step 3.

STEP 3   Choose a newly labelled vertex in Y, say y_i, and label with (y_i) all unlabelled vertices in X joined to y_i by an edge IN M.

Repeat this for all newly labelled vertices in Y.

Repeat Steps 2 and 3 until

EITHER   a vertex in Y which is not incident with an edge in M is labelled (this is called *breakthrough*), in which case go to Part B, Step 4,

OR   no such vertex exists, in which case STOP: the current matching is a maximum matching.

Part B: matching improvement procedure

STEP 4   Find an alternating path as follows.

Start at the breakthrough vertex, and go to the vertex indicated by its label. From this vertex, go to the vertex indicated by *its* label, and so on, until a vertex labelled (∗) is reached.

This path P is an alternating path.

STEP 5   Form a new matching from:

- the edges of the current matching M which are NOT IN the alternating path P;

- the edges of the alternating path P which are NOT IN the current matching M.

Remove all labels and return to Part A, Step 1 to see whether the new matching can be improved further.

Now listen to band 1 of Audio-tape 3.

2.3   Maximum matchings and maximum flows

The problem of finding a maximum matching in a bipartite graph is closely related to the problem of finding a maximum flow in a network. In fact, a problem of finding a maximum matching can always be formulated as a maximum flow problem. To see how this is done, consider the following diagram.

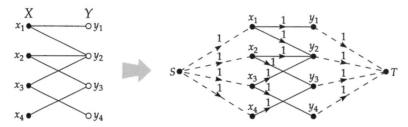

The bipartite graph on the left is converted to a basic network as follows:

- add a source S and a sink T;

- replace each edge $x_i y_j$ by an arc of capacity 1 directed from x_i to y_j;

- for each of the vertices x_i of X, add an arc Sx_i with capacity 1;

- for each of the vertices y_j of Y, add an arc $y_j T$ with capacity 1.

Suppose that we use the maximum flow algorithm to find a maximum flow in this network, as described in *Networks 1*. Then the flow along each arc will have the value 0 or 1.

Furthermore, no two of the arcs shown as solid lines which then have a *flow* of 1 will meet at the same vertex, since the flow into any vertex of X or out of any vertex of Y cannot be greater than 1. It follows that, when the procedure of the algorithm has been carried out, the solid arcs with a flow of 1 in the network correspond to the edges of a maximum matching in the original bipartite graph.

In the diagram, the numbers on the arcs are *capacities*, not *flows*.

In other words, we can solve a maximum matching problem on a bipartite graph by converting the bipartite graph to a basic network, and using the maximum flow algorithm to find a maximum flow. In fact, the algorithm we gave above for finding a maximum matching is a special case of the maximum flow algorithm.

Problem 2.3

In the above diagram, find (by inspection) a maximum matching in the bipartite graph and a corresponding maximum flow in the network. Which feature of the graph corresponds to the capacity of a minimum cut in the network?

We can also obtain the marriage theorem by a similar construction and using the max-flow min-cut theorem of *Networks 1*.

2.4 Computer activities

The computer activities for this section are given in the *Computer Activities Booklet*.

After studying this section, you should be able to:

- explain the term *alternating path* with respect to a matching in a bipartite graph and identify such paths;

- explain briefly the procedure used in the algorithm for finding a maximum matching in a bipartite graph;

- use the algorithm to find a maximum matching in a bipartite graph.

---

3 Assignment problem

In the previous section we were concerned with finding a matching with the maximum possible number of edges in a bipartite graph. Often, there are several such maximum matchings. Sometimes we are concerned with finding just one maximum matching, and we have no reason to prefer one maximum matching to any other. However, if the bipartite graph represents a practical problem, some of the matchings may represent more desirable solutions to the problem than others. We can express this fact by assigning *costs* to the edges of the bipartite graph — we then look for a maximum matching with the lowest total cost. This type of problem is called an **assignment problem**. Let us look at an example.

In Section 4 we shall have weights on both edges and vertices. To distinguish between the two, we refer to the weights on edges as *costs*.

Example 3.1

Three people apply for three jobs. The ability of each applicant for each job is represented by a cost — the lower the cost, the better the ability of the candidate to do the job. We can represent this situation by the following bipartite graph.

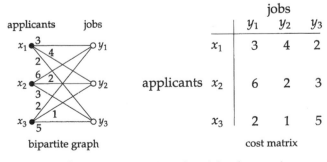

	jobs		
	y_1	y_2	y_3
x_1	3	4	2
applicants x_2	6	2	3
x_3	2	1	5

bipartite graph   cost matrix

We have written the cost associated with the assignment of each applicant to each job next to the corresponding edge. Thus, for example, the cost associated with assigning the applicant x_1 to the job y_2 is 4. For larger graphs it is more convenient to display these costs in the form of a **cost matrix**. The cost matrix for this example is shown to the right of the bipartite graph. ∎

The problem is to find a maximum matching for which the sum of the costs on the edges of the matching is a minimum. One way of proceeding would be to use the exhaustion method — to find all possible maximum matchings and then to choose one with minimum total cost. However, this is not an efficient procedure: for a graph with a large number of vertices, it would take a long time, even using a computer. What is needed is an efficient algorithm. Such an algorithm — called the *Hungarian algorithm* — is given below.

The algorithm is called 'Hungarian' in recognition of the Hungarian mathematician E. Egerváry who introduced the idea in 1931.

In the above example, the number of people is equal to the number of jobs, and the graph is a complete bipartite graph. Other assignment problems may involve incomplete graphs or different numbers of vertices in the two sets. The algorithm we give can accommodate such problems, although it may not be possible to assign all the people to jobs.

3.1 Hungarian algorithm for the assignment problem

The algorithm starts with no initial matching in the bipartite graph containing the sets of vertices $X = \{x_1, x_2, ..., x_n\}$ and $Y = \{y_1, y_2, ..., y_n\}$. It selects a set of edges of the graph in such a way that a matching involving these edges is at minimum cost; that is, it is not possible to find a matching of the same size involving other edges of the graph with a lower total cost. The graph containing the original vertices, together with this set of edges, is called a **partial graph**. If the matching involving the largest possible number of edges in the partial graph is not a maximum matching of the original graph, then further edges are selected and a larger matching is found. This process is repeated until a maximum matching at minimum cost is found.

Note that for this algorithm, the sets X and Y have the *same* number of elements.

The algorithm is in three parts.

First, the first revised cost matrix and first partial graph are constructed.

Parts A and B are essentially the same as in the algorithm for finding a maximum matching given in Section 2.

In the following audio-tape session, we illustrate the use of this algorithm by working through an example. Before listening to the tape, read through the formal statement of the algorithm given here. Have this statement and the *Audio-tape Notes* to hand when you listen to the tape.

Hungarian algorithm for the assignment problem

START   with no initial matching in a bipartite graph whose sets of vertices are $X = \{x_1, x_2, ..., x_n\}$ and $Y = \{y_1, y_2, ..., y_n\}$.

Construction of first partial graph

STEP 0a   Assign weights to the vertices as follows.

> To each vertex of X, assign a weight equal to the lowest cost on any edge incident to that vertex.
>
> Decrease the cost on each edge by the weight on the vertex to which it is incident.
>
> Repeat this procedure for each vertex in Y.

STEP 0b   Construct a partial graph consisting of the vertices of the original bipartite graph, together with only those edges whose current cost is zero.

You can think of an original edge cost as being the total cost of a trip from one vertex to the other. We are dividing this cost into three parts: the cost of leaving the vertex in X; the cost of the journey (the new edge cost); and the cost of arriving at the vertex in Y.

When Step 0a has been carried out, for any edge, the sum of the weights on the end vertices plus the new cost is equal to the original cost.

Part A: labelling procedure

STEP 1 Label with (∗) each vertex in X which is not incident with any edge in the current matching M.

Note that the first time we meet Step 1 the current matching has no edges.

If no such vertex exists, STOP: the current assignment is an optimum assignment.

Otherwise, go to Step 2.

STEP 2 Choose a newly labelled vertex in X, say x_i, and label with (x_i) all the unlabelled vertices in Y joined to x_i by an edge NOT IN M.

Repeat this for all newly labelled vertices in X.

If no vertex in Y is labelled, STOP: the current assignment is an optimum assignment.

Otherwise, go to Step 3.

STEP 3 Choose a newly labelled vertex in Y, say y_i, and label with (y_i) all unlabelled vertices in X joined to y_i by an edge IN M.

Repeat this for all newly labelled vertices in Y.

Repeat Steps 2 and 3 until

EITHER a vertex in Y which is not incident with an edge in M is labelled (this is called *breakthrough*), in which case go to Part B, Step 4,

OR no more labelling is possible, in which case go to Part C, Step 6.

Part B: matching improvement procedure

STEP 4 Find an alternating path as follows.

Start at the breakthrough vertex, and go to the vertex indicated by its label. From this vertex, go to the vertex indicated by *its* label, and so on, until a vertex labelled (∗) is reached.

This path P is an alternating path.

STEP 5 Form a new matching from:

- the edges of the current matching M which are NOT IN the alternating path P;

- the edges of the alternating path P which are NOT IN the current matching M.

Remove all labels and return to Part A, Step 1 to see whether the new matching can be improved further.

Part C: modification of partial graph procedure

STEP 6 Find the lowest current cost on any edge of the original bipartite graph which

- starts at a LABELLED vertex in X;

- ends at an UNLABELLED vertex in Y.

Call this lowest cost δ.

STEP 7 (a) Increase the weight on each labelled vertex in X by δ.

(b) Decrease the weight on each labelled vertex in Y by δ.

(c) For each edge of the original bipartite graph which joins a labelled vertex in X to an unlabelled vertex in Y, decrease the current cost by δ.

(d) For each edge of the original bipartite graph which joins an unlabelled vertex in X to a labelled vertex in Y, increase the current cost by δ.

Note that δ is always positive. Also, the total cost of a 'trip' from a vertex in X to a vertex in Y via any edge, that is, the sum of the two vertex weights and the edge cost, is kept constant throughout Step 7.

Part (c) above will have produced at least one more edge with current cost zero. Incorporate all such edges with zero cost in the partial graph, remove any edge which now has a non-zero cost, delete all labels, and return to Part A, Step 1.

This completes the description of the Hungarian algorithm. It is instructive at this point to compare this algorithm and the algorithm for finding a maximum matching given in the previous section with the maximum flow algorithm described in *Networks 1*. As we pointed out in Section 2, the problem of finding a maximum matching in a bipartite graph is closely related to the problem of finding a maximum flow in a network. The process of finding an alternating path is essentially the same as that of finding a flow-augmenting path in the maximum flow algorithm. The algorithms for these two problems find a flow or a matching at minimum cost, and then increase the flow or the matching in stages, using a procedure which ensures that the cost is a minimum at each stage. Such a procedure is called a **least-cost flow-augmenting cycle**.

Now listen to band 2 of Audio-tape 3.

Remark Some people prefer not to draw the partial graphs when working through the algorithm and instead record everything on the cost matrices. This is very simple to do; the edges of the partial graph correspond to zero entries in the cost matrix, and those zero entries in the matrix corresponding to a matching in the partial graph are indicated by underlining them. The labels required during the labelling procedure can also be indicated on the matrix by placing them by the vertex labels.

Use of dummy vertices

Unlike the maximum matching algorithm and the Hungarian algorithm for the transportation problem, the Hungarian algorithm for the assignment problem as stated above works only when the two sets X and Y have the same number of elements. However, given a problem in which this condition is not satisfied, it is possible to solve the problem by including **dummy vertices** in the initial bipartite graph. The following worked problem illustrates the method.

Worked problem 3.1

A building contractor advertises five jobs — those of bricklayer, carpenter, decorator, electrician and plumber. There are four applicants 1, 2, 3 and 4 — one for carpenter and decorator, one for bricklayer, carpenter and plumber, one for decorator, electrician and plumber, and one for carpenter and electrician.

This is Example 3.6 of the *Introduction* unit.

The applicants have different abilities to do the various jobs, as shown in the following cost matrix — the lower the cost, the more able is the applicant to do that particular job.

		jobs				
		b	c	d	e	p
	1	–	3	2	–	–
	2	4	5	–	–	2
applicants	3	–	–	4	6	3
	4	–	1	–	5	–

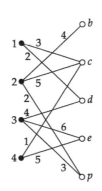

Use the Hungarian algorithm to assign each applicant to a job in such a way that the total cost is a minimum.

Solution

In order to apply the algorithm, we introduce a dummy applicant 5 with the same ability to do each job. Since, in the final solution, we do not wish to assign applicant 5 to a job, we take the corresponding cost to be larger than those of the genuine applicants; let us take this cost to be 20.

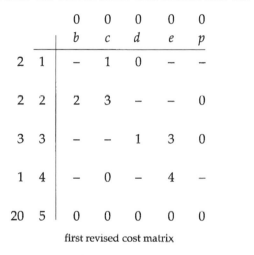

		jobs				
		b	c	d	e	p
applicants	1	–	3	2	–	–
	2	4	5	–	–	2
	3	–	–	4	6	3
	4	–	1	–	5	–
	5	20	20	20	20	20

cost matrix   bipartite graph

We now apply the algorithm in the usual way, ignoring the cells with no entries in the cost matrices.

> We can think of these non-entries as very large costs which do not affect the calculations.

We construct the first revised cost matrix and the first partial graph.

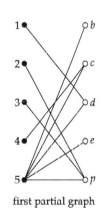

		0	0	0	0	0
		b	c	d	e	p
2	1	–	1	0	–	–
2	2	2	3	–	–	0
3	3	–	–	1	3	0
1	4	–	0	–	4	–
20	5	0	0	0	0	0

first revised cost matrix   first partial graph

By inspection, we find a matching with four edges: let us choose the edges

$1d, \quad 2p, \quad 4c, \quad 5b.$

Part A

We carry out the labelling procedure and do not achieve breakthrough.

Part C

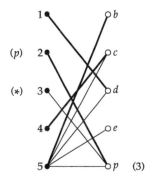

We revise the cost matrix as follows.

		0	0	0	0	0
		b	c	d	e	p
2	1	−	1	0	−	−
2	2	2	3	−	−	0
3	3	−	−	1	3	0
1	4	−	0	−	4	−
20	5	0	0	0	0	0

We find that $\delta = 1$.

We obtain the following revised cost matrix and revised partial graph.

		0	0	0	0	−1
		b	c	d	e	p
2	1	−	1	0	−	−
3	2	1	2	−	−	0
4	3	−	−	0	2	0
1	4	−	0	−	4	−
20	5	0	0	0	0	1

We carry out the labelling procedure and do not achieve breakthrough.

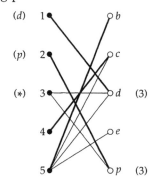

Part C

We revise the cost matrix as follows.

		0	0	0	0	−1
		b	c	d	e	p
2	1	−	1	0	−	−
3	2	1	2	−	−	0
4	3	−	−	0	2	0
1	4	−	0	−	4	−
20	5	0	0	0	0	1

We find that $\delta = 1$.

We obtain the following revised cost matrix and revised partial graph.

		0	0	-1	0	-2
		b	c	**d**	e	**p**
3	1	–	0	0	–	–
4	2	0	1	–	–	0
5	3	–	–	0	1	0
1	4	–	0	–	4	–
20	5	0	0	1	0	2

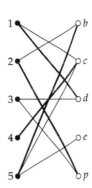

Part A

We carry out the labelling procedure and achieve breakthrough at e.

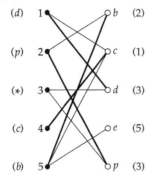

Part B

An alternating path is $3p2b5e$.

We obtain the following revised matching.

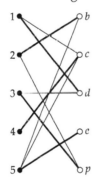

Part A

No vertex in X can be labelled, so we STOP.

We now ignore the dummy applicant 5.

Thus an optimum assignment is

      1–decorator, 2–bricklayer, 3–plumber, 4–carpenter

with total cost

      $(3 + 0 - 1) + (4 + 0 + 0) + (5 + 0 - 2) + (1 + 0 + 0) = 10$

calculated from the final revised cost matrix, or

      $2 + 4 + 3 + 1 = 10$

calculated from the original cost matrix. ∎

3.2 Bottleneck assignment problem

Many problems which occur in practice are variations of the basic assignment problem, and can be solved by modifying the Hungarian algorithm. We now give an example of such a problem, called the **bottleneck assignment problem**, and show how the basic algorithm can be adapted to solve it.

Suppose that a product is to be made on a serial production line which involves a number of activities, each of which must be completed once to produce one item of the product. A number of people are to be assigned to these activities. If we know how long it takes each person to complete each activity, how can we assign the people to the activities so that the time taken to complete one item of the product is as short as possible?

It is clear that the production line can operate only as fast as the rate of working of the slowest person on the line — the *bottleneck*. What we need to do, therefore, is to find an assignment of people to activities such that the longest time taken by any person to do his or her assigned activity is a minimum. In the following worked problem, we show how to solve such a problem by modifying the algorithm for the assignment problem so that, instead of finding a maximum matching at minimum *total* cost, we find a maximum matching for which the largest *individual* cost (in this case the time taken by the slowest worker) is a minimum.

'The time taken to complete one item of the product' is ambiguous here. What is meant is the time interval between two items rolling off the production line. This is not the total sum of the times for the various activities, because the workers are working on the activities at the same time.

Worked problem 3.2

Suppose that three people are to be assigned to three activities on a production line, and that the times (in minutes) taken for the people to do the various activities are given by the following cost matrix.

		activity		
		y_1	y_2	y_3
	x_1	3	2	2
person	x_2	3	4	3
	x_3	2	2	1

How can we assign the three people to the three activities in such a way that the production line can operate as quickly as possible?

Solution

We denote the time taken to complete one item of the product by p, so that, in a particular assignment of people to activities, p is the longest time taken by any one person to do his or her assigned activity. At each stage of the modified algorithm for this problem, we need to keep account only of the parameter p. This makes the procedure considerably simpler than that of the algorithm for the basic assignment problem, where at each stage we have to keep account of the *total* cost, which we do by assigning weights to all the vertices of the graph.

Note that when we have a partial assignment, the current value of p will be the longest time taken by any person to do the activities assigned to him or her so far.

The lowest cost in the above cost matrix is 1, corresponding to worker x_3 doing activity y_3. We set p initially to this value, because it cannot be lower, and subtract 1 from all the entries in the cost matrix.

This gives a new cost matrix from which we can construct the corresponding partial graph, as we did in the assignment problem, using only those entries in the cost matrix which are zero. The new cost matrix and partial graph corresponding to $p = 1$ are as follows.

	y_1	y_2	y_3
x_1	2	1	1
x_2	2	3	2
x_3	1	1	0

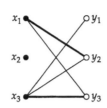

The partial graph has only one edge, so a maximum matching comprises just this edge, shown by a thick line. A complete assignment has not been found, so we must enlarge the partial graph. The minimum of all the non-zero costs is 1, so we reduce the costs of all non-zero entries in the matrix by 1 and increase the value of p by the same amount. This gives the following cost matrix and partial graph, corresponding to $p = 2$.

	y_1	y_2	y_3
x_1	1	0	0
x_2	1	2	1
x_3	0	0	0

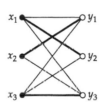

We can now include the edge $x_1 y_2$ in the matching, so this is shown by a thick line.

Again, a complete assignment has not been found, so we continue updating the cost matrix, finding the minimum non-zero entry (again 1) and reducing each non-zero entry by this amount and increasing p by the same amount. This gives the following cost matrix and partial graph, corresponding to $p = 3$.

	y_1	y_2	y_3
x_1	0	0	0
x_2	0	1	0
x_3	0	0	0

We can now include the edge $x_2 y_1$ in the matching, so this is shown by a thick line. A complete assignment has now been made, and so the minimum time for the completion of one item is 3 minutes (the final value of p). ∎

Note that there are other possible optimum matchings in the final partial graph corresponding to alternative optimum assignments.

We state the algorithm formally as follows.

Algorithm for the bottleneck assignment problem

START   with a given cost matrix.

   Set $p = 0$.

STEP 1   (a) Set d = smallest non-zero entry in current cost matrix.

   (b) Reduce each non-zero entry in the current cost matrix by d.

   (c) Increase p by d.

STEP 2   Use the matching algorithm to find a maximum matching in the bipartite graph.

   If a complete assignment is achieved, STOP: this is an optimum assignment and the value of p is the required answer.

   Otherwise, return to STEP 1.

The simple example in the above worked problem is chosen to illustrate only the *modifications* to the assignment algorithm. Thus in Step 2 we found a maximum matching *by inspection* each time. For a more complicated example, in Step 2 it is necessary to find an alternating path with respect to the existing matching and use it to obtain a maximum matching.

Four people are to be assigned to four activities on a serial production line. The times (in minutes) taken for the people to do the various activities are as follows.

		activity			
		y_1	y_2	y_3	y_4
	x_1	3	1	5	10
person	x_2	7	4	2	3
	x_3	8	8	5	2
	x_4	8	8	5	2

Assign the four people to the four activities in such a way that the production line can operate as quickly as possible.

3.3 Computer activities

The computer activities for this section are described in the *Computer Activities Booklet*.

> After studying this section, you should be able to:
>
> - explain what is meant by the *assignment problem* and the *bottleneck assignment problem*;
>
> - explain briefly the procedure of the Hungarian algorithm for the assignment problem and how it can be modified to solve the bottleneck assignment problem;
>
> - solve simple examples of the assignment problem and the bottleneck assignment problem.

4 Transportation problem

The well-known transportation problem, sometimes called the *Hitchcock problem* after F. L. Hitchcock, who studied the problem in 1941, can be stated as follows.

> **Transportation problem**
>
> A manufacturer has a number of factories, each of which can supply a particular product to a number of warehouses. Each factory has a fixed output, and there is a transportation cost involved in sending the product from each factory to each warehouse. To which warehouses should the products of each factory be sent so that the requirements of all the warehouses are satisfied at minimum total cost?

Example 4.1

An example of the transportation problem involving three factories and four warehouses is represented by the following bipartite graph. The costs of supplying each warehouse from each factory are given in the cost matrix to the right of the graph.

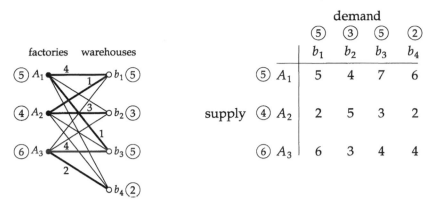

demand				
	(5) b_1	(3) b_2	(5) b_3	(2) b_4
(5) A_1	5	4	7	6
supply (4) A_2	2	5	3	2
(6) A_3	6	3	4	4

In the bipartite graph, the factories A_1, A_2 and A_3 are represented by the black vertices, which we call **supply vertices**. The warehouses b_1, b_2, b_3 and b_4 are represented by the white vertices, which we call **demand vertices**.

The circled numbers next to the supply and demand vertices on the graph, and also on the cost matrix, are the numbers of units of the product supplied by the factories or demanded at the warehouses. In this example, the total supply and the total demand are both 15 units.

Note that for a solution to be possible, the total supply must be at least as large as the total demand.

A flow pattern which satisfies the supply and demand constraints is indicated by the thick edges of the bipartite graph. The number beside each of these edges is the number of units of the product to be sent along the route represented by that edge. The other edges represent unused routes. We can calculate the total transportation cost for this flow pattern by multiplying the amount of flow along each edge by the cost associated with that edge. Thus the total cost is

$$(4 \times 5) + (1 \times 7) + (1 \times 2) + (3 \times 5) + (4 \times 4) + (2 \times 8) - 68.$$

Although this flow pattern satisfies the flow constraints, it is not a minimum-cost solution. ∎

We ask you to find a minimum-cost solution by using an algorithm in Problem 4.1.

The transportation problem is closely related to the assignment problem which we discussed in the previous section. If, in the assignment problem, we interpret the assignment of a worker to a job as being a 'flow' of one unit between the corresponding vertices of the bipartite graph representation, then we see that the assignment problem is a special case of the transportation problem in which the supplies and demands at the vertices are all 1. The transportation problem is more complicated, because we need to specify the amount of flow along each edge included in a solution, and also because a single supply vertex (factory) may send goods to more than one demand vertex (warehouse).

The Hungarian algorithm for the transportation problem which we give in this section is based on the algorithm for the assignment problem.

4.1 Hungarian algorithm for the transportation problem

Before setting down the detailed procedure of the algorithm, we describe the method in general terms.

The first step is to construct a partial graph, using the same procedure as in the algorithm for the assignment problem. We then assign the maximum possible flow to the edges of the partial graph, subject to the supply and demand constraints at each vertex. The way in which the partial graph is constructed ensures that this is a minimum-cost flow — in other words, we cannot obtain the same value of the total flow at a lower cost by using edges not in the partial graph. If the flow thus obtained does not satisfy the demands at all the demand vertices, then we enlarge the partial graph, using the same procedure as in the algorithm for the assignment problem. We can then increase the value of the total flow by using the new edges. We continue in this way until we eventually obtain a minimum cost solution in which all the demands are satisfied. It is important to note that, as with the assignment problem, there may be other minimum-cost solutions.

The Hungarian algorithm thus builds up the flow in stages, ensuring that at each stage the total flow is at a minimum cost — thus it uses a least-cost flow-augmenting cycle.

In the Hungarian algorithm for the transportation problem, we are not seeking a matching, as we were in the algorithm for the assignment problem. (This is because there may be flows from one supply vertex to a number of demand vertices.) So, instead of looking for alternating paths, we look for paths in which there is a flow on *even* edges — that is, on the 2nd, 4th, 6th, ... edges. There may or may not be a flow on odd edges of the path.

Such a path is analogous to a flow-augmenting path used in the maximum flow algorithm in *Networks 1*.

In the following audio-tape session, we illustrate the use of this algorithm by working through an example. Before listening to the tape, read through the description given below. Have this description and the *Audio-tape Notes* to hand when you listen to the tape.

Hungarian algorithm for the transportation problem

START with no flow in a bipartite graph whose vertices are divided into two sets: the supply vertices $A_1, ..., A_n$ and the demand vertices $b_1, ..., b_m$.

Construction of initial partial graph

STEP 0a Assign weights to the supply and demand vertices as follows.

To each supply vertex, assign a weight equal to the lowest cost on any edge incident with that vertex.

Decrease the cost on each edge by the weight on the supply vertex with which it is incident.

Repeat this for each demand vertex.

STEP 0b Construct a partial graph consisting of the vertices of the original bipartite graph, together with only those edges whose current cost is zero.

Part A: labelling procedure

STEP 1 Label with (∗) each supply vertex whose supply has not all been allocated to edges.

If no such vertex exists, STOP: the current solution is a minimum-cost solution.

Otherwise, go to Step 2.

STEP 2 Choose a newly labelled supply vertex A_i, and label with (A_i) all unlabelled demand vertices which are joined by an edge of the partial graph.

Repeat this for all newly labelled supply vertices, and then go to Step 3.

STEP 3 Choose a newly labelled demand vertex b_j, and label with (b_j) all unlabelled supply vertices which are joined to b_j by an edge which has been allocated a flow.

Repeat this for all newly labelled demand vertices.

Repeat Steps 2 and 3 until

EITHER a demand vertex whose demand is not satisfied is labelled (this is called *breakthrough*), in which case go to Part B, Step 4,

OR no more labelling is possible, in which case go to Part C, Step 6.

Part B: flow-augmenting procedure

STEP 4 Start with the breakthrough vertex, and trace back through the labels until a supply vertex which is labelled (∗) is reached. A flow-augmenting path has been found.

The flow-augmenting path plays a similar role in this algorithm to that of the alternating path in the algorithm for the assignment problem.

Calculate the maximum flow F which can be sent along this path as follows.

First, find the minimum of all flows assigned to EVEN edges of the path (that is, the 2nd, 4th, ... edges). This is the maximum possible backward flow.

Next, find the minimum value of:

Note that for a flow-augmenting path with just one edge, there is no backward flow, so we just take the minimum of the supply and the demand.

- the available supply at the start vertex of the path;

- the required demand at the end vertex;

- the maximum backward flow.

This is the required value of F.

STEP 5 Form a new flow pattern as follows.

(i) Increase the flows on the ODD edges of the path by this value of flow, F.

Decrease the flows on the EVEN edges by F.

(ii) Decrease the available supply at the START vertex by F.

Decrease the demand at the END vertex by F.

Remove all the labels and return to Part A, Step 1.

Part C: modification of partial graph procedure

STEP 6 Find the lowest current cost on any edge of the original bipartite graph which

- starts at a LABELLED supply vertex;

- ends at an UNLABELLED demand vertex.

Call this lowest cost δ.

STEP 7 (a) Increase the weight on each labelled supply vertex by δ.

(b) Decrease the weight on each labelled demand vertex by δ.

(c) For each edge which joins a labelled supply vertex to an unlabelled demand vertex, decrease the current cost by δ.

(d) For each edge which joins an unlabelled supply vertex to a labelled demand vertex, increase the current cost by δ.

Incorporate all edges which now have a current cost of zero in the partial graph, remove any edge which now has a non-zero cost, delete all labels, and return to Part A, Step 1.

Now listen to band 3 of Audio-tape 3.

Problem 4.1

Use the Hungarian algorithm to find a minimum-cost solution to the transportation problem described in the text at the beginning of this section, and calculate the total transportation cost. The cost matrix is repeated in the margin.

		demand			
		⑤	③	⑤	②
		b_1	b_2	b_3	b_4
	⑤ A_1	5	4	7	6
supply	④ A_2	2	5	3	2
	⑥ A_3	6	3	4	4

Use of a dummy vertex

In each of the examples of the transportation problems which we have considered, the total supply is equal to the total demand. In other cases, the total supply may be greater than the total demand — for example, in the previous problem it may be a simple matter to increase the supply of each factory by 2 units. To enable us to use the Hungarian algorithm to solve such problems, we introduce a **dummy vertex**. This represents an artificial warehouse (or other demand vertex) whose demand is chosen to be equal to the excess supply. Thus, for the example of Problem 4.1, if each factory can supply 2 additional units and the warehouse demands are the same, we represent the problem by the following bipartite graph and cost matrix.

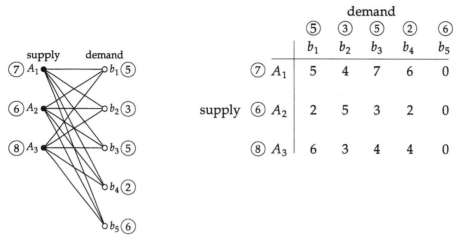

		demand			
	⑤	③	⑤	②	⑥
	b_1	b_2	b_3	b_4	b_5
⑦ A_1	5	4	7	6	0
supply ⑥ A_2	2	5	3	2	0
⑧ A_3	6	3	4	4	0

Vertex b_5 is the dummy vertex with an artificial demand of 6, equal to the excess supply. In the cost matrix, we must set the transportation costs from each supply vertex to this dummy vertex to be equal — we have chosen here to set them all equal to 0. We can then apply the algorithm in the usual way. The flow pattern produced will send 6 units to the dummy vertex. To obtain a flow pattern which is a solution to the original problem, we simply remove all flows to the dummy vertex.

4.2   Transhipment problem

In the transportation problem discussed above, we assumed that the products from each factory are sent directly to one or more warehouses. However, in a practical situation, it may be cheaper to send the products from a factory first to an intermediate point (one of the other factories or warehouses) and then on to the destination warehouse.

The sending of goods via intermediate points is called **transhipment**, and a problem in which transhipment is allowed is called a *transportation problem with transhipment*, or, more simply, a **transhipment problem**. The graphical representation of a transhipment problem is not a bipartite graph, since we can send goods from factory to factory, or from warehouse to warehouse. However, we can easily transform the graphical representation into a bipartite graph — to do this, we represent each factory or warehouse by two vertices, one representing the factory or warehouse as a supply point, and one representing it as a demand point. To illustrate how this works, we consider a specific example.

Example 4.2

Suppose we have a transportation problem for which the transportation costs are as shown in the following cost matrix, in which the circled numbers are the amounts of supply or demand at the vertices.

	demand		
	(5)	(4)	(6)
	b_1	b_2	b_3
(2) A_1	15	11	15
supply (6) A_2	17	14	11
(7) A_3	18	18	15

If transhipment is allowed, then there are costs associated with the various transhipment routes. We suppose that these are as given in the following cost matrix.

	demand					
	(0)	(0)	(0)	(5)	(4)	(6)
	a_1	a_2	a_3	b_1	b_2	b_3
(2) A_1	0	6	5	15	11	15
(6) A_2	5	0	4	17	14	11
(7) A_3	4	4	0	18	18	15
(0) B_1	14	19	20	0	5	4
(0) B_2	10	12	17	5	0	2
(0) B_3	17	13	14	4	2	0

supply

In this matrix, A_1 represents the first factory considered as a supply vertex, and a_1 represents the same factory considered as a demand vertex. Similarly, B_1 represents the first warehouse considered as a supply vertex, and b_1 represents that warehouse considered as a demand vertex. Since we must consider each factory and warehouse as both demand and supply vertices, we have a total of six supply vertices and six demand vertices. Note that the part of the cost matrix for the original vertices A_1, A_2, A_3 and b_1, b_2, b_3 is the same as the original cost matrix.

As before, the circled numbers indicate the amounts demanded or available at the vertices considered as demand or supply vertices. Factories considered as demand vertices have zero demand, and warehouses considered as supply vertices have zero supply. The fact that the cost matrix is not symmetric means that outgoing shipments and returning shipments do not cost the same. The entries on the diagonal of the matrix are all zero, since they are the costs of transporting goods between supply and demand vertices which represent the same factory or warehouse. ∎

By splitting the vertex representing each factory or warehouse into two vertices — a supply vertex and a demand vertex — we have cast the transportation problem with transhipment into the same form as a transportation problem without transhipment. We do this so that we can apply the Hungarian algorithm for the transportation problem to the problem with transhipment. However, before we can apply the algorithm, a further modification is required. The reason for this is the following. When we apply the Hungarian algorithm, we can ship goods from a demand vertex to a supply vertex only if there is already a flow from that supply vertex to that demand vertex. This means that, for the transportation problem with transhipment, we cannot ship goods from a particular factory considered as a demand vertex to the same factory considered as a supply vertex. To overcome this problem, we add to all the supplies and demands an amount of demand or supply at least as great as the total demand or supply. This ensures that any vertex considered as a demand vertex can accommodate any transhipment which could occur in the solution to the problem. When the algorithm has been completed, we remove these artificial supplies and demands (and the corresponding artificial flows) to obtain a solution to the original problem.

Worked problem

Use the Hungarian algorithm for the transportation problem to obtain a minimum-cost solution to the above transhipment problem.

Solution

The total supply and the total demand are both equal to 15. We add an amount greater than this to all the supplies and demands — we choose 20 as the amount to be added.

When we apply the algorithm, we form a partial graph, using the cost matrix given in the above text. Since all the entries on the main diagonal are zero, and all other entries are non-zero, this partial graph consists only of the edges joining A_1 to a_1, A_2 to a_2, and so on, as follows.

$$(22)\ A_1 \bullet\!\!-\!\!\!-\!\!\!-\!\!\!-\!\!\!-\!\!\!-\!\!\circ a_1\ (20)$$

$$(26)\ A_2 \bullet\!\!-\!\!\!-\!\!\!-\!\!\!-\!\!\!-\!\!\circ a_2\ (20)$$

$$(27)\ A_3 \bullet\!\!-\!\!\!-\!\!\!-\!\!\!-\!\!\!-\!\!\circ a_3\ (20)$$

$$(20)\ B_1 \bullet\!\!-\!\!\!-\!\!\!-\!\!\!-\!\!\!-\!\!\circ b_1\ (25)$$

$$(20)\ B_2 \bullet\!\!-\!\!\!-\!\!\!-\!\!\!-\!\!\!-\!\!\circ b_2\ (24)$$

$$(20)\ B_3 \bullet\!\!-\!\!\!-\!\!\!-\!\!\!-\!\!\!-\!\!\circ b_3\ (26)$$

The labelling procedure and the procedure for modifying the flow pattern result in a flow of 20 being sent along each edge — these are the artificial flows necessary to ensure that any transhipment can be accommodated. The resulting flow pattern is shown below. The circled numbers next to the vertices represent unallocated supplies or unsatisfied demands — these are just the original supplies and demands.

$$(2)\ A_1 \bullet\overset{20}{-\!\!\!-\!\!\!-\!\!\!-\!\!\!-}\circ a_1\ (0)$$

$$(6)\ A_2 \bullet\overset{20}{-\!\!\!-\!\!\!-\!\!\!-\!\!\!-}\circ a_2\ (0)$$

$$(7)\ A_3 \bullet\overset{20}{-\!\!\!-\!\!\!-\!\!\!-\!\!\!-}\circ a_3\ (0)$$

$$(0)\ B_1 \bullet\overset{20}{-\!\!\!-\!\!\!-\!\!\!-\!\!\!-}\circ b_1\ (5)$$

$$(0)\ B_2 \bullet\overset{20}{-\!\!\!-\!\!\!-\!\!\!-\!\!\!-}\circ b_2\ (4)$$

$$(0)\ B_3 \bullet\overset{20}{-\!\!\!-\!\!\!-\!\!\!-\!\!\!-}\circ b_3\ (6)$$

We continue to apply the algorithm in the same way as for a transportation problem without transhipment: the procedure is exactly the same as that used in the first worked problem. We thus obtain the following flow pattern.

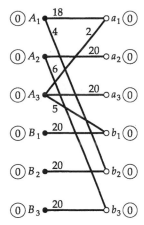

The flow path $A_3 a_1 A_1 b_2$ involves transhipment via the factory A_1. To accommodate the flow of 2 along this path, the artificial flow along the edge $A_1 a_1$ has been reduced from 20 to 18. No other flow path involves transhipment.

To obtain the flow pattern which is a solution to the original problem, we must subtract all the artificial flows of 20 from the flow pattern given above. This gives the following solution, in which we have indicated the direction of flow along each edge by an arrow. The original supplies and demands are shown next to the vertices.

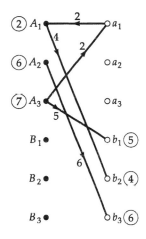

4.3 Computer activities

The computer activities for this section are described in the *Computer Activities Booklet*.

After studying this section, you should be able to:

(a) explain what is meant by the *transportation problem* and the *transhipment problem*;

(b) explain briefly the procedure used in the Hungarian algorithm for the transportation problem;

(c) find a minimum-cost solution to simple examples of the transportation and transhipment problems by applying the Hungarian algorithm.

Further reading

Discussion of the material in Sections 1 and 2 is included in many books on combinatorics — for example:

J. O. Clark and D. A. Holton, *A First Look at Graph Theory*, World Scientific Publishing, 1991;

G. Chartrand and O. R. Oellerman, *Applied and Algorithmic Graph Theory*, McGraw-Hill, 1993;

R. J. Wilson, *Introduction to Graph Theory*, 4th edition, Longman Group, 1996;

C. L. Liu, *Introduction to Combinatorial Mathematics*, McGraw-Hill, 1968.

Most books on network theory include a section dealing with aspects of the topics of Sections 3 and 4 — for example:

L. R. Ford, Jr. and D. R. Fulkerson, *Flows in Networks*, Princeton University Press, 1962;

E. Lawler, *Combinatorial Optimization: Networks and Matroids*, Holt, Rinehart and Winston, 1976.

Exercises

Section 1

Matching problem

1.1 Five people have each won a holiday to one of five resorts — Blackpool, Cannes, Edinburgh, Paris and San Francisco. Of the winners, one will go only to Britain, one will not go to France or Scotland, two will not go to Britain, and the fifth will go only to San Francisco.

(a) Draw the bipartite graph representing this situation.

(b) By finding a maximum matching in this graph (by inspection), determine whether it is possible for each winner to go to a different resort.

1.2 A computer agency advertises for a systems analyst (S), a programmer (P) and a computer manager (M). There are four applicants — one is a qualified systems analyst (A_1), two are both qualified systems analysts and programmers (A_2 and A_3), and the other is a qualified programmer and computer manager (A_4).

(a) Draw up a table showing, for each possible subset of jobs, the number of jobs in that subset and the number of suitable applicants for that subset of jobs.

(b) For each subset, indicate whether the marriage condition is satisfied, and decide whether it is possible for all three jobs to be filled.

(c) Draw the bipartite graph representing this situation and find, by inspection, a maximum matching in this graph corresponding to the maximum number of jobs that can be filled.

1.3 Does there exist a maximum matching containing 4 edges in the following bipartite graph? If so, find such a matching; if not, explain why such a matching does not exist.

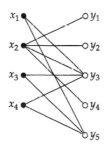

1.4 Five tutors T_1, T_2, T_3, T_4, T_5 apply to teach five courses; just one tutor is required for each course. To find out how many of the tutors can be appointed to courses which they are competent to teach, the marriage theorem is applied to each subset of tutors. It is found that the marriage condition is satisfied for all except the following subsets:

tutors T_1, T_2 and T_3 are between them competent to teach only 2 courses;

tutors T_1 and T_3 are between them competent to teach only 1 course.

(a) How many of the five tutors can simultaneously be appointed to courses which they are competent to teach? Explain your answer.

(b) For which of the following subsets can all the tutors in the subset be appointed to courses which they are competent to teach? Explain your answer.

    (1) $\{T_1, T_2, T_3, T_4\}$ (2) $\{T_2, T_3, T_4\}$

    (3) $\{T_1, T_2, T_4, T_5\}$ (4) $\{T_1, T_3, T_5\}$

    (5) $\{T_1, T_2, T_3, T_5\}$ (6) $\{T_1, T_3, T_4, T_5\}$

1.5 A university has 5 vacancies V_1, V_2, V_3, V_4, V_5, and there are 5 applicants A_1, A_2, A_3, A_4, A_5, whose suitability for the different jobs is shown in the following table.

job	suitable applicants
V_1	A_1, A_2, A_3
V_2	A_3, A_4
V_3	A_4
V_4	A_4
V_5	A_1, A_2, A_5

(a) Draw a bipartite graph to represent this situation.

(b) List all the subsets of vacancies for which the marriage condition is not satisfied.

(c) For each of these subsets, find the value of the expression in the modified marriage theorem, and hence find the largest number of vacancies which can be filled.

(d) Find, by inspection, a matching in the bipartite graph with this number of edges.

Section 2

Maximum matching algorithm

2.1 Find, by inspection, an alternating path in the following bipartite graph, and hence obtain a new matching with one more edge.

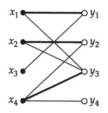

2.2 Carry out the labelling procedure for the graph in Exercise 2.1.

2.3 Consider the following labelled bipartite graph.

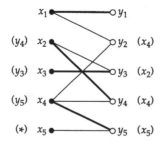

Starting from the breakthrough vertex, trace back through the labels to find an alternating path, and hence obtain a new matching with one more edge.

2.4 Use the maximum matching algorithm to find a maximum matching in the following bipartite graph, starting from the given initial matching.

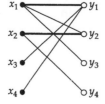

Section 3

Hungarian algorithm for the assignment problem

3.1 Construct the first revised cost matrix from the original cost matrix given below, and draw the corresponding partial graph.

	y_1	y_2	y_3	y_4
x_1	4	6	8	3
x_2	2	5	1	4
x_3	6	5	3	2
x_4	3	4	4	1

3.2 For the following partial graph and current cost matrix, find the lowest non-zero current cost δ and construct the revised cost matrix.

	0	1	2	0
	y_1	y_2	y_3	y_4
5 x_1	0	3	0	1
3 x_2	4	2	0	0
4 x_3	3	0	2	4
2 x_4	5	0	4	5

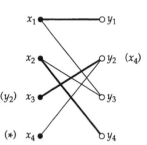

3.3 Four candidates apply for four jobs. The selection committee rates the suitability of each candidate for each job and expresses this as a cost, where the lower the cost, the more suitable is that candidate for that job. Allocate the candidates to the jobs in such a way that the total cost is as small as possible, using the Hungarian algorithm. The costs are as follows.

		jobs			
		y_1	y_2	y_3	y_4
	x_1	3	1	5	10
applicants	x_2	7	4	2	3
	x_3	8	8	5	2
	x_4	8	8	5	2

Bottleneck assignment problem

3.4 Four people are to be assigned to four activities on a serial production line. The times (in minutes) taken for the people to do the various jobs are as follows.

		activities			
		y_1	y_2	y_3	y_4
	x_1	1	3	4	8
people	x_2	4	4	3	3
	x_3	7	8	3	1
	x_4	6	4	5	3

Use an appropriate algorithm to assign the four people to the four activities in such a way that the production line can operate as quickly as possible.

Section 4

Hungarian algorithm for the transportation problem

4.1 Given the following partial graph of a transportation problem, carry out the labelling procedure.

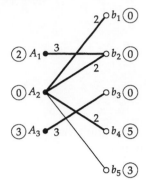

4.2 Three factories, A_1, A_2 and A_3, can supply 10, 15 and 20 units of product, respectively. The demands for these products at four warehouses, b_1, b_2, b_3 and b_4, are 5, 12, 13 and 15 units, respectively. The costs of transporting one unit of product from each factory to each warehouse are given in the following cost matrix.

	b_1	b_2	b_3	b_4
A_1	25	10	2	30
A_2	5	15	20	10
A_3	80	65	0	2

Find a minimum-cost solution to this transportation problem, using the Hungarian algorithm.

4.3 Describe briefly how you would modify your solution to Exercise 4.2 if the supply at factory A_2 were 18, rather than 15.

Transhipment problem

4.4 A transhipment problem has the following cost matrix.

		demand		
	⓪	⓪	③	②
	a_1	a_2	b_1	b_2
② A_1	0	1	3	4
③ A_2	1	0	4	6
⓪ B_1	6	4	0	1
⓪ B_2	5	3	1	0

supply (label on left of the matrix)

Use the Hungarian algorithm to find a minimum-cost solution, and determine the value of this minimum cost.

Solutions to the exercises

1.1

(a) The bipartite graph representing this situation is:

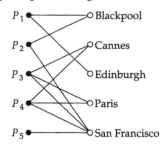

(b) There are only two maximum matchings:

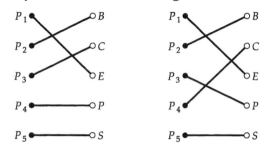

These matchings show two ways in which all five winners can go to different resorts.

1.2

(a)

subset of jobs	applicants	number of jobs	number of applicants
$\{S, P, M\}$	A_1, A_2, A_3, A_4	3	4
$\{S, P\}$	A_1, A_2, A_3, A_4	2	4
$\{S, M\}$	A_1, A_2, A_3, A_4	2	4
$\{P, M\}$	A_2, A_3, A_4	2	3
$\{S\}$	A_1, A_2, A_3	1	3
$\{P\}$	A_2, A_3, A_4	1	3
$\{M\}$	A_4	1	1

(b) The marriage condition is satisfied for every subset, so, by the marriage theorem, all three jobs can be filled by suitable applicants.

(c) The bipartite graph representing this situation is shown below. A maximum matching of three edges is indicated by three thick lines. Other matchings with three edges are possible.

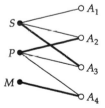

1.3 There is no maximum matching containing four edges in this bipartite graph because each of the vertices x_1, x_3 and x_4 is joined only to the vertices y_3 and y_5.

1.4

(a) Only four tutors can simultaneously be appointed to courses which they are competent to teach, because only T_2, T_4, T_5 and *one* of T_1 and T_3 can be appointed.

(b) The sets containing only *one* of T_1 and T_3 — namely, sets (2) and (3).

1.5

(a) The bipartite graph representing this situation is:

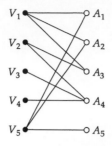

(b) The subsets of vacancies for which the marriage condition is not satisfied are listed below:

vacancies	applicants	number of vacancies m	number of applicants p
$\{V_2, V_3, V_4\}$	A_3, A_4	3	2
$\{V_3, V_4\}$	A_4	2	1

(c) For each of these subsets, the expression $p + (n - m)$ in the modified marriage theorem has value 4, and so the largest number of vacancies that can be filled by suitable applicants is 4.

(d) Both subsets of vacancies for which the marriage condition is not satisfied contain the vacancies V_3 and V_4. Therefore, if we remove one of the vacancies V_3 and V_4, the remaining vacancies can be filled. A solution is shown in the following diagram.

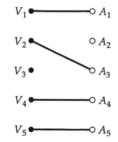

Other solutions are possible.

2.1 The only alternating path is $x_3\, y_1\, x_1\, y_3\, x_4\, y_4$.

To obtain the new matching, we take the edges of the alternating path NOT IN M — that is, $x_3\, y_1$, $x_1\, y_3$ and $x_4\, y_4$ — together with the edges of M NOT IN the alternating path — that is, $x_2\, y_2$. This gives the matching shown in the margin.

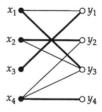

2.2 We carry out the following steps.

STEP 1 Label with (∗) each vertex in X which is not incident with any edge in the current matching M — that is, x_3.

STEP 2 Label with (x_3) all unlabelled vertices in Y joined to x_3 by an edge NOT IN M — that is, y_1.

STEP 3 Label with (y_1) all unlabelled vertices in X joined to y_1 by an edge IN M — that is, x_1.

STEP 2 Label with (x_1) all unlabelled vertices in Y joined to x_1 by an edge NOT IN M — that is, y_3.

STEP 3 Label with (y_3) all unlabelled vertices in X joined to y_3 by an edge IN M — that is, x_4.

STEP 2 Label with (x_4) all unlabelled vertices in Y joined to x_4 by an edge NOT IN M — that is, y_2 and y_4.

Breakthrough occurs at y_4, so the labelling procedure terminates.

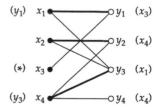

Note that if we trace back through the labels from the breakthrough vertex y_4 we obtain the alternating path in Solution 2.1.

2.3 The breakthrough vertex is y_2. Tracing back through the labels from y_2, we obtain the alternating path $x_5\ y_5\ x_4\ y_2$.

The new matching is obtained from the existing one by replacing the edge $x_4\ y_5$ by the edges $x_4\ y_2$ and $x_5\ y_5$, as follows.

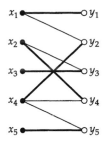

2.4 Applying the labelling procedure, we obtain one of the following labelled graphs.

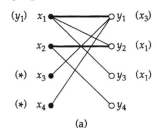 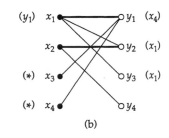

In each case, breakthrough occurs at y_3.

In case (a), an alternating path is $x_3\ y_1\ x_1\ y_3$.

In case (b), an alternating path is $x_4\ y_1\ x_1\ y_3$.

We thus obtain one of the following new matchings.

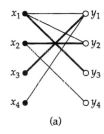 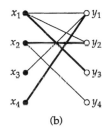

Applying the labelling procedure again, we obtain one of the following labelled graphs.

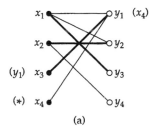 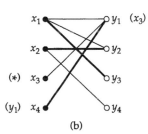

Breakthrough is not achieved in either case, so we STOP.

Thus a maximum matching has three edges, as shown above.

The point of the exercise is to demonstrate how the algorithm terminates. However, in this small example it is clear from the graph that a maximum matching has only three edges, since the vertices A_3 and A_4 are joined only to b_1.

3.1 The lowest cost of any edge incident with x_1 is 3, so we give x_1 weight 3 and reduce the cost of all the entries in row x_1 by 3. Similarly, we reduce rows x_2, x_3 and x_4 by their lowest costs 1, 2 and 1, respectively. The matrix becomes

		y_1	y_2	y_3	y_4
3	x_1	1	3	5	0
1	x_2	1	4	0	3
2	x_3	4	3	1	0
1	x_4	2	3	3	0

Next we consider the columns. Column y_1 has lowest cost 1, column y_2 has lowest cost 3, and columns y_3 and y_4 each have lowest cost 0. For each column, we subtract the lowest cost from each entry in that column, and the revised cost matrix becomes

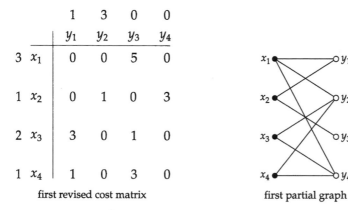

		1	3	0	0
		y_1	y_2	y_3	y_4
3	x_1	0	0	5	0
1	x_2	0	1	0	3
2	x_3	3	0	1	0
1	x_4	1	0	3	0

first revised cost matrix   first partial graph

The corresponding partial graph, consisting of all the vertices together with the edges with zero current cost, is shown above on the right.

3.2 We start with the following situation, and apply Part C of the Hungarian algorithm for the assignment problem.

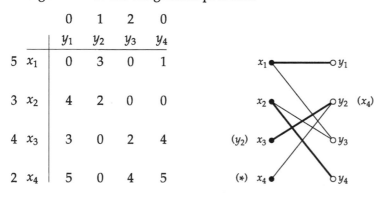

		0	1	2	0
		y_1	y_2	y_3	y_4
5	x_1	0	3	0	1
3	x_2	4	2	0	0
4	x_3	3	0	2	4
2	x_4	5	0	4	5

STEP 6   We draw a horizontal line through each labelled vertex in X.

We draw a vertical line through each labelled vertex in Y.

		0	1	2	0
		y_1	y_2	y_3	y_4
5	x_1	0	3	0	1
3	x_2	4	2	0	0
4	x_3	3	0	2	4
2	x_4	5	0	4	5

44

The smallest entry with only a horizontal line through it is min $(3, 2, 4, 5)$, so $\delta = 2$.

STEP 7   We *decrease* all entries with only a *horizontal* line through them by 2, and *increase* the weights on the corresponding vertices in X by 2.

We *increase* all entries with only a *vertical* line through them by 2, and *decrease* the weights on the corresponding vertices in Y by 2.

We thus obtain the revised cost matrix.

		0	-1	2	0
		y_1	y_2	y_3	y_4
5	x_1	0	5	0	1
3	x_2	4	4	0	0
6	x_3	1	0	0	2
4	x_4	3	0	2	3

3.3   We apply the algorithm as follows.

We construct the first revised cost matrix and the first partial graph.

		2	0	0	0
		y_1	y_2	y_3	y_4
1	x_1	0	0	4	9
2	x_2	3	2	0	1
2	x_3	4	6	3	0
2	x_4	4	6	3	0

Part A

By inspection, we find a matching with three edges: let us choose $x_1 y_1$, $x_2 y_3$ and $x_3 y_4$. We label the first partial graph as follows.

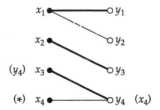

Breakthrough is not achieved, so we go to Part C.

Part C

		2	0	0	0
		y_1	y_2	y_3	y_4
1	x_1	0	0	4	9
2	x_2	3	2	0	1
2	x_3	4	6	3	0
2	x_4	4	6	3	0

We find that $\delta = \min (4, 6, 3) = 3$.

We obtain the following revised cost matrix and revised partial graph.

		2	0	0	-3
		y_1	y_2	y_3	y_4
1	x_1	0	0	4	12
2	x_2	3	2	0	4
5	x_3	1	3	0	0
5	x_4	1	3	0	0

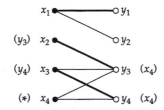

Part A

We label the revised partial graph as follows.

$$
\begin{array}{l}
x_1 \\
(y_3)\ x_2 \\
(y_4)\ x_3 \\
(*)\ x_4
\end{array}
\qquad
\begin{array}{l}
y_1 \\
y_2 \\
y_3\ (x_4) \\
y_4\ (x_4)
\end{array}
$$

Breakthrough is not achieved, so we go to Part C.

Part C

		2	0	0	-3
		y_1	y_2	y_3	y_4
1	x_1	0	0	4	12
2	x_2	3	2	0	4
5	x_3	1	3	0	0
5	x_4	1	3	0	0

We find that $\delta = \min (3, 2, 1) = 1$.

We obtain the following revised cost matrix and revised partial graph.

		2	0	-1	-4
		y_1	y_2	y_3	y_4
1	x_1	0	0	5	13
3	x_2	2	1	0	4
6	x_3	0	2	0	0
6	x_4	0	2	0	0

Part A

We label the revised partial graph as follows.

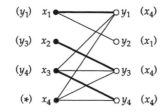

We have breakthrough at vertex y_2.

Tracing back through the labels from y_2, we obtain the alternating path $x_4 y_1 x_1 y_2$.

We form a new matching as follows.

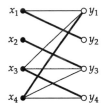

A complete assignment has been found at a total cost of

$$1 + 2 + 2 + 8 = 13,$$

obtained from the original cost matrix, or

$$(1 + 0 + 0) + (3 + 0 - 1) + (6 + 0 - 4) + (6 + 0 + 2) = 13,$$

obtained from the final revised cost matrix.

Other matchings with this lowest value for the total cost are possible.

3.4 The lowest cost in the cost matrix is 1, so we set $p = 1$ and subtract 1 from all the entries in the cost matrix. This gives the following cost matrix and partial graph, corresponding to $p = 1$.

	y_1	y_2	y_3	y_4
x_1	0	2	3	7
x_2	3	3	2	2
x_3	6	7	2	0
x_4	5	3	4	2

The partial graph has only two edges, joining different pairs of vertices, so a maximum matching comprises these two edges, shown by thick lines.

A complete assignment has not been found, so we repeat the process. The lowest non-zero cost is 2, so we subtract 2 from all the non-zero entries in the cost matrix, and increase p by 2. This gives the following cost matrix and partial graph, corresponding to $p = 3$.

	y_1	y_2	y_3	y_4
x_1	0	0	1	5
x_2	1	1	0	0
x_3	4	5	0	0
x_4	3	1	2	0

An alternating path is $x_4 y_4 x_3 y_3$, which leads to the matching

$$x_1 y_1, \quad x_3 y_3, \quad x_4 y_4.$$

A complete assignment has not been found, so we repeat the process. The lowest non-zero cost is 1, so we subtract 1 from all the non-zero entries in the cost matrix, and increase p by 1. This gives the following cost matrix and partial graph, corresponding to $p = 4$.

	y_1	y_2	y_3	y_4
x_1	0	0	0	4
x_2	0	0	0	0
x_3	3	4	0	0
x_4	2	0	1	0

An alternating path is $x_2 y_1 x_1 y_2$, which leads to the complete assignment

$$x_1 y_2, \quad x_2 y_1, \quad x_3 y_3, \quad x_4 y_4.$$

The minimum time for completion of an item is 4 minutes (the final value of p).

4.1 We start with the following situation.

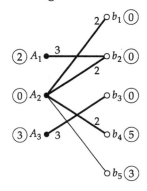

We carry out the following steps.

STEP 1   The supplies at the supply vertices A_1 and A_3 have not all been allocated, so we label A_1 and A_3 with (∗).

STEP 2   The newly labelled supply vertex A_1 is joined to b_2 and the newly labelled supply vertex A_3 is joined to b_3, so we label b_2 with (A_1) and b_3 with (A_3).

STEP 3   The newly labelled demand vertex b_2 is joined to the unlabelled supply vertex A_2 by an edge which has been allocated a flow, so we label A_2 with (b_2).

          All supply vertices are now labelled.

STEP 2   The newly labelled supply vertex A_2 is joined to the unlabelled demand vertices b_1, b_4 and b_5. We label b_1 with (A_2) and b_4 with (A_2). The demand at b_4 is not satisfied, so breakthrough occurs at b_4 and the labelling procedure terminates.

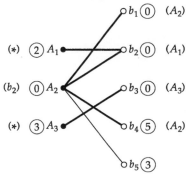

We start with the following situation.

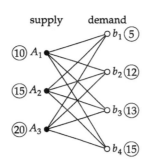

We construct the first revised cost matrix and first partial graph.

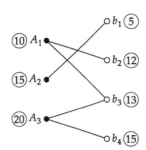

Parts A and B

Following the procedure of Steps 1–5, we find a maximum flow in the above partial graph. We thus obtain the following flow pattern.

Other maximum flows are possible.

The edges carrying a flow are shown as thick lines. We have indicated the amounts of flow, and have subtracted these amounts from the supplies and demands at the appropriate vertices.

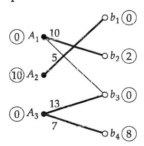

Part A

We label A_2 with $(*)$ and b_1 with (A_2).

The partial graph with these labels is shown below.

The current cost matrix is repeated to the left of the graph.

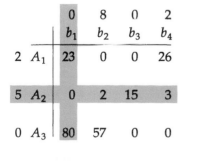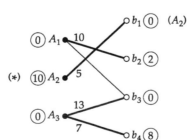

No more labelling is possible, and breakthrough has not been achieved, so we go to Part C.

Part C

We find that $\delta = \min (2, 15, 3) = 2$.

We thus obtain the following revised cost matrix and partial graph.

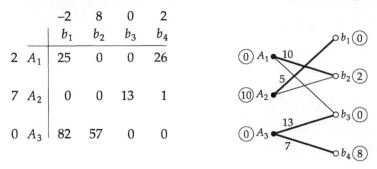

| | | −2 | 8 | 0 | 2 |
		b_1	b_2	b_3	b_4
2	A_1	25	0	0	26
7	A_2	0	0	13	1
0	A_3	82	57	0	0

Part A

We label the partial graph as follows.

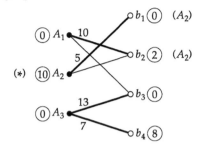

Breakthrough is achieved at b_2, so we go to Part B.

Part B

A flow-augmenting path is $A_2 b_2$. There is no flow along this edge.

The available supply at the start vertex A_2 is 10 and the required demand at the end vertex b_2 is 2, so we send a flow of 2 along $A_2 b_2$.

This results in the following flow pattern.

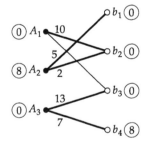

Part A

We label the partial graph as follows.

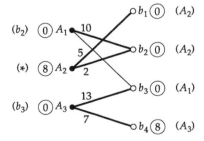

Breakthrough is achieved at b_4, so we go to Part B.

Part B

Tracing back through the labels from b_4, we find the flow-augmenting path $A_2 b_2 A_1 b_3 A_3 b_4$.

The even edges are $A_1 b_2$ and $A_3 b_3$ with flows of 10 and 13 respectively, and min $(10, 13) = 10$. Thus the maximum possible backward flow is 10.

The available supply at A_2 is 8.

The required demand at b_4 is 8.

The maximum flow F is therefore equal to min $(10, 8, 8) = 8$.

Sending a flow of 8 along the flow-augmenting path $A_2 b_2 A_1 b_3 A_3 b_4$, we obtain the following flow pattern.

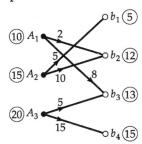

4.3 We introduce a dummy vertex b_5 with demand equal to 3, the excess supply. The vertex b_5 is joined, in the bipartite graph, to the supply vertices A_1, A_2, and A_3, and the corresponding entries in the cost matrix are set equal to each other. We then apply the algorithm in the usual way, and obtain the solution of the original problem by simply ignoring all flows to the dummy vertex.

4.4 We start with the following situation.

		demand			
		⓪	⓪	③	②
		a_1	a_2	b_1	b_2
	② A_1	0	1	3	4
	③ A_2	1	0	4	6
supply	⓪ B_1	6	4	0	1
	⓪ B_2	5	3	1	0

The total supply and the total demand are both equal to 5. We add 5 to all the supplies and demands.

When we apply the algorithm, we form a partial graph, using the cost matrix given above. Since all the entries on the main diagonal are zero, and all other entries are non-zero, this partial graph consists only of the edges joining A_1 to a_1, A_2 to a_2, and so on, as follows. (We have omitted the circled numbers representing supplies and demands from the cost matrices.)

		0	0	0	0
		a_1	a_2	b_1	b_2
0	A_1	0	1	3	4
0	A_2	1	0	4	6
0	B_1	6	4	0	1
0	B_2	5	3	1	0

⑦ A_1 ●————○ a_1 ⑤

⑧ A_2 ●————○ a_2 ⑤

⑤ B_1 ●————○ b_1 ⑧

⑤ B_2 ●————○ b_2 ⑦

51

Parts A and B

This results in a flow of 5 being sent along each edge — these are the artificial flows necessary to ensure that any transhipment can be accommodated. The resulting flow pattern is shown below. The circled numbers next to the vertices represent unallocated supplies or unsatisfied demands — these are just the original supplies and demands.

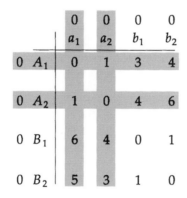

Part A

We label A_1 and A_2 with $(*)$.

We label a_1 with (A_1) and a_2 with (A_2).

No more labelling is possible, and breakthrough has not been achieved, so we go to Part C.

Part C

		0	0	0	0
		a_1	a_2	b_1	b_2
0	A_1	0	1	3	4
0	A_2	1	0	4	6
0	B_1	6	4	0	1
0	B_2	5	3	1	0

We find that $\delta = \min(3, 4, 6) = 3$.

We thus obtain the following revised cost matrix and partial graph.

		−3	−3	0	0
		a_1	a_2	b_1	b_2
3	A_1	0	1	0	1
3	A_2	1	0	1	3
0	B_1	9	7	0	1
0	B_2	8	6	1	0

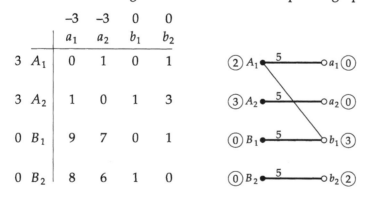

Part A

We label A_1 and A_2 with $(*)$.

We label a_1 and b_1 with (A_1).

Breakthrough is achieved at b_1, so we go to Part B.

Part B

We send a flow of 2 along the flow-augmenting path $A_1 b_1$.

This results in the following flow pattern.

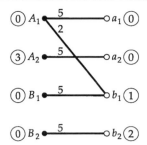

Part A

We label A_2 with $(*)$.

We label a_2 with (A_2).

No more labelling is possible, and breakthrough has not been achieved, so we go to Part C.

Part C

		a_1	a_2	b_1	b_2
		-3	-3	0	0
3	A_1	0	1	0	1
3	A_2	1	0	1	3
0	B_1	9	7	0	1
0	B_2	8	6	1	0

We find that $\delta = \min (1, 3) = 1$.

We thus obtain the following revised cost matrix and partial graph.

		a_1	a_2	b_1	b_2
		-3	-4	0	0
3	A_1	0	2	0	1
4	A_2	0	0	0	2
0	B_1	9	8	0	1
0	B_2	8	7	1	0

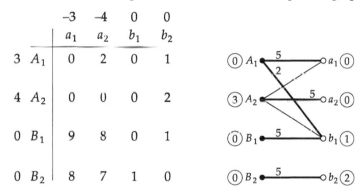

Part A

We label A_2 with $(*)$.

We label a_1, a_2 and b_1 with (A_2).

Breakthrough is achieved at b_1, so we go to Part B.

Part B

We send a flow of 1 along the flow-augmenting path $A_2 b_1$.

This results in the following flow pattern.

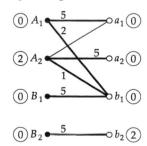

Part A

We label A_2 with $(*)$.

We label a_1, a_2 and b_1 with (A_2).

We label A_1 with (a_1) and B_1 with (b_1).

No more labelling is possible, and breakthrough has not been achieved, so we go to Part C.

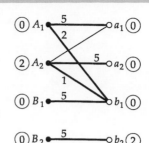

Part C

		-3	-4	0	0
		a_1	a_2	b_1	b_2
3	A_1	0	2	0	1
4	A_2	0	0	0	2
0	B_1	9	8	0	1
0	B_2	8	7	1	0

We find that $\delta = \min(1, 2) = 1$.

We thus obtain the following revised cost matrix and partial graph.

		-4	-5	-1	0
		a_1	a_2	b_1	b_2
4	A_1	0	2	0	0
5	A_2	0	0	0	1
1	B_1	9	8	0	0
0	B_2	9	8	2	0

Part A

We label A_2 with $(*)$.

We label a_1, a_2 and b_1 with (A_2).

We label A_1 with (a_1) and B_1 with (b_1).

We label b_2 with (A_1).

Breakthrough is achieved at b_2, so we go to Part B.

Part B

Tracing back through the labels from b_2, we find a flow-augmenting path $A_2 a_1 A_1 b_2$.

There are other flow-augmenting paths.

The even edge $A_1 a_1$ has a flow of 5. Thus the maximum possible backward flow is 5.

The available supply at A_2 is 2.

The required demand at b_2 is 2.

The maximum flow F is therefore $\min(5, 2, 2) = 2$.

We send a flow of 2 along each of the odd edges $A_2 a_1$ and $A_1 b_2$.

We decrease the flow on the even edge $A_1 a_1$ from 5 to 3.

We thus obtain the following flow pattern.

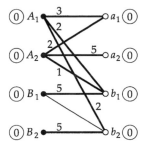

The flow path $A_2 a_1 A_1 b_1$ involves transhipment via the factory A_1. To accommodate the flow of 2 along this path, the artificial flow along the edge $A_1 a_1$ has been reduced from 5 to 3. No other flow path involves transhipment.

To obtain the flow pattern which is a solution to the original problem, we must subtract all the artificial flows of 5 along $A_1 a_1$, $A_2 a_2$, $B_1 b_1$ and $B_2 b_2$ from the flow pattern given above. This gives the following solution, in which we have indicated the direction of flow along each edge by an arrow. The original supplies and demands are shown next to the vertices.

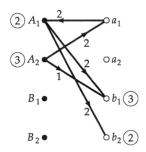

The total transportation cost is obtained by multiplying the value of the flow along each edge by the original cost associated with that edge. Thus the total transportation cost is

$$(2 \times 1) + (2 \times 3) + (1 \times 4) + (2 \times 4) = 20.$$

Solutions to the problems

Solution 1.1

(a) The bipartite graph representing this situation is given below.

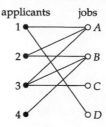

(b) The only matching containing four edges is the following.

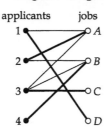

This is a maximum matching, since there are clearly no matchings with more than four edges. The matching shows how all four applicants can be assigned to jobs for which they are qualified.

Solution 1.2

(a)

subset of men	women known	number of men	number of women known	Is marriage condition satisfied?
$\{A_1, A_2, A_3\}$	B_1, B_2, B_3, B_4	3	4	yes
$\{A_1, A_2\}$	B_1, B_3, B_4	2	3	yes
$\{A_1, A_3\}$	B_1, B_2, B_3, B_4	2	4	yes
$\{A_2, A_3\}$	B_2, B_3, B_4	2	3	yes
$\{A_1\}$	B_1, B_3, B_4	1	3	yes
$\{A_2\}$	B_4	1	1	yes
$\{A_3\}$	B_2, B_3	1	2	yes

The marriage condition is satisfied for every subset, so, by the marriage theorem, all three men can marry women they know.

(b) The number of non-empty subsets of a set of size n is $2^n - 1$. For this problem, $n = 3$, so we need to consider $2^3 - 1 = 7$ subsets — this agrees with the number of entries in the table.

(c) The bipartite graph representing this situation is shown below. A maximum matching of three edges (corresponding to all three men being able to marry women they know) is indicated by thick lines.

Other matchings with three edges are possible.

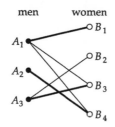

Solution 1.3

(a) The bipartite graph representing this situation is:

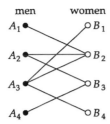

(b) The only subset of men for which the marriage condition is not satisfied is the subset $\{A_1, A_2, A_4\}$ which contains three men who collectively know only two women, B_2 and B_3.

(c) Since we know from part (b) that the marriage condition is not satisfied, the marriage theorem tells us that not all of the four men can marry women they know. It follows that, if we can find a matching containing three edges, then this is a maximum matching. There are several such matchings, two of which are:

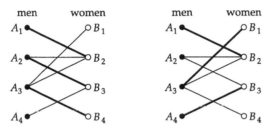

Since a maximum matching contains three edges, the maximum number of men who can marry women they know is three.

Solution 1.4

(a) The marriage condition is clearly not satisfied, since the five men between them know only four women.

(b) The bipartite graph representing this situation is:

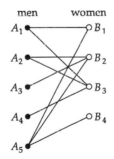

(c) The subsets of men for which the marriage condition is not satisfied are listed below, together with the value of the expression $p + (n - m)$ in the modified marriage theorem.

subset of men	women known	number of men m	number of women known p	$p + (n - m)$
$\{A_2, A_3, A_4\}$	B_2, B_3	3	2	4
$\{A_1, A_2, A_3, A_4\}$	B_1, B_2, B_3	4	3	4
$\{A_1, A_2, A_3, A_4, A_5\}$	B_1, B_2, B_3, B_4	5	4	4

(d) From the above table, we see that the minimum value of the expression $p + (n - m)$ in the modified marriage theorem is 4. By the theorem, the largest number of men who can marry women they know is 4.

All the subsets of men for which $p + (n - m)$ is equal to its minimum value of 4 contain the men A_2, A_3 and A_4. It follows that if we add one additional woman B_5 who knows any one of these men, then the marriage condition is satisfied for all possible subsets. Therefore, if we remove any one of A_2, A_3 and A_4, then the remaining four men will be able to marry women they know from the original four women. The list of subsets of four men who can all marry women they know is therefore:

$$\{A_1, A_3, A_4, A_5\}, \quad \{A_1, A_2, A_4, A_5\}, \quad \{A_1, A_2, A_3, A_5\}.$$

Solution 2.1

(a) The path $x_3 \, y_2 \, x_2 \, y_1$ is not an alternating path, since the initial vertex x_3 and the final vertex y_1 are both incident with edges in M.

(b) The path $y_3 \, x_3 \, y_2 \, x_2 \, y_1 \, x_1$ is an alternating path.

(c) The path $x_3 \, y_4 \, x_4 \, y_3$ is not an alternating path, since the initial vertex x_3 is incident with an edge in M.

Solution 2.2

There are six alternating paths:

$x_3 \, y_3 \, x_2 \, y_1 \, x_1 \, y_2,$ $x_3 \, y_4 \, x_4 \, y_5,$ $x_5 \, y_4 \, x_4 \, y_5,$ $x_3 \, y_4 \, x_4 \, y_3 \, x_2 \, y_1 \, x_1 \, y_2,$

$x_5 \, y_4 \, x_4 \, y_3 \, x_2 \, y_1 \, x_1 \, y_2,$ $x_3 \, y_2.$

Solution 2.3

Let us start with the matching shown by thick lines in the bipartite graph below.

Applying the labelling procedure, we obtain the following labelled graph.

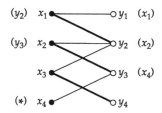

Breakthrough occurs at y_1. Tracing back through the labels from y_1, we obtain the alternating path $x_4 \, y_3 \, x_2 \, y_2 \, x_1 \, y_1$.

We thus obtain the improved matching shown on the left below and a corresponding maximum flow of value 4 shown in the network on the right. This is the flow which we would obtain by applying the maximum flow algorithm to the given network.

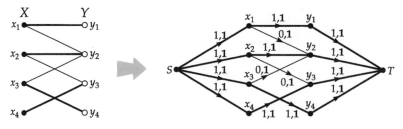

The number of edges in a maximum matching in the graph is equal to the capacity of a minimum cut in the network.

Solution 3.1

The lowest cost in the cost matrix is 1, so we set $p = 1$ and subtract 1 from all the entries in the cost matrix. This gives the following cost matrix and partial graph, corresponding to $p = 1$.

	y_1	y_2	y_3	y_4
x_1	2	0	4	9
x_2	6	3	1	2
x_3	7	7	4	1
x_4	7	7	4	1

The partial graph has only one edge, so a maximum matching comprises just this edge, shown by a thick line.

A complete assignment has not been found, so we repeat the process. The lowest non-zero cost is 1, so we subtract 1 from all the non-zero entries in the cost matrix. This gives the following cost matrix and partial graph, corresponding to $p = 2$.

	y_1	y_2	y_3	y_4
x_1	1	0	3	8
x_2	5	2	0	1
x_3	6	6	3	0
x_4	6	6	3	0

We can now include the edges $x_2 y_3$ and $x_3 y_4$ in the matching.

A complete assignment has not been found, so we repeat the process, giving the following cost matrix and partial graph, corresponding to $p = 3$.

	y_1	y_2	y_3	y_4
x_1	0	0	2	7
x_2	4	1	0	0
x_3	5	5	2	0
x_4	5	5	2	0

There are no alternating paths in the partial graph, so the matching cannot be improved.

A complete assignment is still not possible, so we repeat the process, giving the following cost matrix and partial graph, corresponding to $p = 4$.

	y_1	y_2	y_3	y_4
x_1	0	0	1	6
x_2	3	0	0	0
x_3	4	4	1	0
x_4	4	4	1	0

There are no alternating paths in the partial graph, so the matching cannot be improved.

A complete assignment is still not possible, so we repeat the process once more, giving the following cost matrix and partial graph, corresponding to $p = 5$.

	y_1	y_2	y_3	y_4
x_1	0	0	0	5
x_2	2	0	0	0
x_3	3	3	0	0
x_4	3	3	0	0

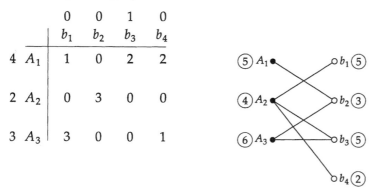

There are two alternating paths in the partial graph:

$$x_4 y_3 x_2 y_2 x_1 y_1 \quad \text{and} \quad x_4 y_4 x_3 y_3 x_2 y_2 x_1 y_1$$

giving the matchings

$$x_1 y_1, x_2 y_2, x_3 y_4, x_4 y_3 \quad \text{and} \quad x_1 y_1, x_2 y_2, x_3 y_3, x_4 y_4,$$

respectively. These are both optimum assignments.

A complete assignment has been achieved, and the minimum time for completion of an item is 5 minutes (the final value of p).

Solution 4.1

The application of the algorithm is outlined below. For convenience, we have omitted the circled numbers representing supplies and demands from the cost matrices.

We assign weights to the vertices, and construct the first revised cost matrix and first partial graph.

		0	0	1	0
		b_1	b_2	b_3	b_4
4	A_1	1	0	2	2
2	A_2	0	3	0	0
3	A_3	3	0	0	1

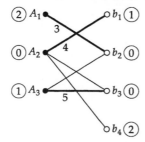

Parts A and B

Following the procedure of Steps 1–5, we find a maximum flow in the above partial graph. We thus obtain the following flow pattern.

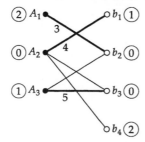

The edges carrying a flow are shown as thick lines. We have indicated the amounts of flow, and have subtracted these amounts from the supplies and demands at the appropriate vertices.

We return to Part A.

Part A

We carry out the labelling procedure. We label vertices A_1 and A_3 with (*), and then label vertex b_2 with (A_1) and vertex b_3 with (A_3).

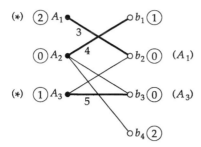

No more labelling is possible, and breakthrough has not been achieved, so we go to Part C.

Part C

		0	0	1	0
		b_1	b_2	b_3	b_4
4	A_1	1	0	2	2
2	A_2	0	3	0	0
3	A_3	3	0	0	1

We find that $\delta = \min(1, 2, 3) = 1$.

We obtain the following revised cost matrix and revised partial graph.

		0	−1	0	0
		b_1	b_2	b_3	b_4
5	A_1	0	0	2	1
2	A_2	0	4	1	0
4	A_3	2	0	0	0

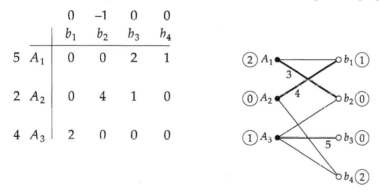

Part A

We carry out the labelling procedure and obtain the following labels on the partial graph.

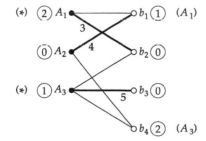

Breakthrough is achieved at b_1, and also at b_4, so we go to Part B.

Part B

The procedure of Steps 6 and 7 results in a flow of 1 being sent from A_1 to b_1, and a flow of 1 being sent from A_3 to b_4. This results in the following flow pattern.

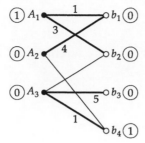

Part A

We carry out the labelling procedure, and thus obtain the following labels on the partial graph.

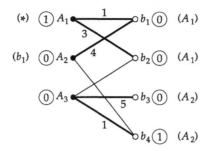

Breakthrough is achieved at b_4, so we go to Part B.

Part B

Tracing back through the labels from b_4, we obtain the flow-augmenting path $A_1 b_1 A_2 b_4$.

The even edge $A_2 b_1$ has a flow of 4. Thus the maximum possible backward flow is 4.

The available supply at A_1 is 1.

The required demand at b_4 is 1.

The maximum flow F is therefore min $(4, 1, 1) = 1$.

We send a flow of 1 along each of the odd edges $A_1 b_1$ and $A_2 b_4$.

We decrease the flow on the even edge $A_2 b_1$ from 4 to 3.

We thus obtain the following flow pattern. The original supplies and demands are shown next to the vertices.

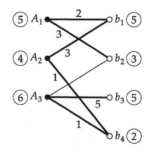

This flow pattern is the required minimum-cost solution.

The total transportation cost is obtained by multiplying the value of the flow along each edge by the original cost associated with that edge. Thus the total transportation cost is

$$(2 \times 5) + (3 \times 4) + (3 \times 2) + (1 \times 2) + (5 \times 4) + (1 \times 4) = 54.$$

Index